CAREER REMIX

DAMON BROWN

STERLING
New York

STERLING
New York

An Imprint of Sterling Publishing Co., Inc.

STERLING and the distinctive Sterling logo are registered trademarks of
Sterling Publishing Co., Inc.

Text © 2022 Damon Brown

ISBN 978-1-4549-4415-7
ISBN 978-1-4549-4416-4 (e-book)

Distributed in Canada by Sterling Publishing Co., Inc.
c/o Canadian Manda Group, 664 Annette Street
Toronto, Ontario M6S 2C8, Canada
Distributed in the United Kingdom by GMC Distribution Services
Castle Place, 166 High Street, Lewes, East Sussex BN7 1XU, England
Distributed in Australia by NewSouth Books
University of New South Wales, Sydney, NSW 2052, Australia

For information about custom editions, special sales, and premium and corporate
purchases, please contact Sterling Special Sales at 800-805-5489 or specialsales@
sterlingpublishing.com.

Manufactured in the United States of America

2 4 6 8 10 9 7 5 3 1

sterlingpublishing.com

Cover design by Elizabeth Mihaltse Lindy
Interior design by Gavin C. Motnyk

"In the midst of chaos, there is also opportunity."

—SUN TZU

DEDICATED TO UNCLE GEORGE, DAD, AND POP—THE ORIGINAL
CAREER REMIXERS. I LOVE Y'ALL.

CONTENTS

THE NOBLE PIG

My Southern African American relatives have a wonderful saying: "From the rooter to the tooter." From our very early time in America, this phrase means utilizing every part of the pig (from the nose, used for rooting out food on the ground, to the behind, used for passing gas). My enslaved ancestors had to work with the scraps, the leftovers, and the discards given after the head family ate the most desired parts. From this, we see the origins of pigs' feet, chitterlings, and ham hocks. Today, they are honored parts of the soul-food catalog, culinary delights spruced up and served by Michelin-star restaurants down South and beyond. But they came from pain, necessity, and, most notably, innovation.

"From the rooter to the tooter" now applies to any situation in which we utilize our whole experience. It means there is nothing wasted. Ironically, this saying derived from the desire for survival, but now it represents a mindset of abundance. *Mindset* author and psychologist Carol Dweck would call this a *growth* mindset, viewing every experience as an abundant opportunity to learn, as opposed to a *fixed* mindset, looking at things as win-or-lose propositions. Dweck says a fixed mindset person believes they have innate abilities: "I am smart at math." It also means they believe in innate caps: "I am dumb at science." They believe themselves, and everyone, to be born into their station in life. They put themselves into an intellectual caste system.

"Dozens of studies later, Dweck's findings suggest that people exhibiting fixed mind-sets tend to gravitate to activities that confirm their abilities, whereas those with growth mind-sets tend to seek activities that expand their abilities," writes Peter Sims, author of *Little Bets: How Breakthrough Ideas Emerge from Small Discoveries.* "Dweck explains, 'When confronted with a task, people with a fixed mind-set ask, 'Am I going to be good at it immediately?' With a growth mind-set, people ask, 'Well, can I learn to do it?' Students with fixed mind-sets want to appear capable, even if that means not learning in the process. Because setback and criticism threaten their self-image, they give up more easily and exhibit greater risk aversion."

This fixed mentality stunts how well we can adapt to career opportunities, recognize our business potential, or otherwise thrive in our professions. How can you upskill, pivot, or evolve if you believe that you are stuck with whatever learning/capacity you currently have? This isn't new: picture the silent film stars unwilling to adapt to the talkie movies or the horse-and-buggy dealers not acknowledging the power of the Model T. No, the real challenge today is twofold.

First, we are the CEO of our own career. From the Baby Boomers on, each new age group has had more independent branding—from social-media posts to the gig economy—and less job security. Baby Boomers are expected to have about a half dozen jobs in their lifetime, and the number has increased about 50 percent for each successive generation (nine jobs for Gen X, and so on).

Second, the needs of the community—that is, the needs of the job market—are changing exponentially faster. Yes, technology is part of the trend, with the Internet, mobile devices, and increased globalization evolving our needs. Deeper than that are our own needs. We want the businesses we patronize to reflect, or at least not offend, our personal ethics, while creating a seemingly tailored experience for us and us alone. And in the workforce, it's not enough to have a long career at one organization—we also want to have work–life balance, be inspired in a stable environment, and make an impact on the world.

It doesn't mean we are asking for too much. It does mean we can't use old methods to create new, fluid careers.

Going to school for several years and paying hundreds of thousands of dollars makes sense when the career path guarantees a return on investment, if not an exponential ROI. Narrowly defining your skill to focus on a specific output makes sense when specialty, not versatility, is king. The best career opportunities today, though, didn't exist yesterday, and identifying too closely with the medium, instead of the message, is a quick way to make yourself extinct.

Chris Jones, innovative food entrepreneur and cofounder of ChefSteps, an online resource for cooks, says, "Growing up, my father told me 'Don't worry about what you're going to do' because the job I was going to do hadn't been invented yet. . . . The most interesting jobs are the ones that you make up. As I shared in my book *The Ultimate Bite-Sized Entrepreneur*, "the best way to strive every day is to actually dive into new circumstances as if they were on your agenda. . . . Uncertainty is your ally. The tools, the skills, and the circumstances you need to make your mark on the world may not even exist yet. You cannot be certain of what's going to happen next. An event that happens in the next twenty-four hours could change the course of your career and provide a quantum leap in your understanding. It will not be something you can predict, and it will not be something you can control. It will be something that you will have to accept. The less resistance you have to your next adventure, the more you will gain from its arrival."

Keep in mind that my previous book and Jones's brilliant commentary came in 2017, well before the coronavirus pandemic. The record-breaking unemployment, radical work-from-home modifications, and evolving market needs accelerated the cycle. People who had mastered in-person networking, speaking, and presentations suddenly had to pivot onto the computer screen. Service workers adapted their environment to socially distant, plastic-glass-buffered experiences. Educators used to facilitating face-to-face intimacy began to see technology not as a nicety, but as a lifeline to their students.

Every single one of us is adjusting. The playing field is about as level as it's going to get in our lifetime. And that window of opportunity is closing.

"Right now, the focus is on being conservative—doing what puts food on your table—and it can be very destructive since the recession won't last forever, but these ideas can become habits," *The 48 Laws of Power* author Robert Greene told me when we were talking during the *last* recession a decade ago. If anything, his evergreen advice proves his point—your career must ride the cycle of constant change. "If you're at a job and you can't leave, you can say, 'I'm going to be prudent and not fearful. I'm going to learn more skills and stay here for two more years,' and it changes the whole game. If you want to start your own business, and I'm a huge proponent of entrepreneurship as that's the only way you have control, then you could be working at Pizza Hut, but at night you're studying or doing another thing where you have a purpose."

In *Career Remix*, we're going to break down three strong traits that will help you maximize the opportunities you've got right now. First, we will recognize the strengths you have on deck. Upskilling, reeducating, and redefining yourself don't make much sense if you don't acknowledge the insight, power, and resources you've already earned. You do not need to throw away your previous or current career to grow. Instead, that will become the fertilizer, if not the advantage, of your next career move. Second, we will design a plan for our next move. It isn't meticulously figuring out your next career. It is becoming clear on the intention, and that intention then becomes the compass. The beauty is that a compass set to true north will always point to the next best move. Better to be fixed on your intention than to orient your career around a leader, organization, or identity. Lastly, we will draw in others who value our true north as much as we do. Networking has gotten a bad rap of late, probably because the emphasis has been on transactional interactions—"I'll do this for you if you do this for me"—instead of relational interactions—"I want to see you grow because we both have the same ultimate intention." Once you connect based on wanting the same impact on the world, then you pull in advocates that want to see you win, gain customers that will happily pay a premium to work with you, and attract leaders who do their best to put you into a position of power.

It isn't about acing the next job interview. It's not about clinging on to a position that isn't working anymore. It isn't about assuming that whatever work you do now will be what you do forever.

It is time to take a holistic approach to your career. Any stumbles, surprises, or strays just add more to your toolbox. Let's dig in and maximize what you've got to make your best career.

From the rooter to the tooter.

→

PART I.
ESTABLISH YOUR NEW NORMAL

You either walk in your story and own your truth, or you live outside of your story, hustling for your worthiness.

—Brené Brown

The quickest way not to get anywhere is to try to go back to what was. You cry over what is finished, overanalyze your past decisions based on the information you have available now, and miss opportunities that are in the here and now. It is what you hear as the next politician gets into office, as the new job replaces the old one, or as vaccines roll out for an epidemic. We want things to go back to normal, as if we hadn't changed in the interim. We want to return to how it was, willfully ignoring any insight—any gifts—delivered to us in the process. We want to turn back time, fooling ourselves into thinking things were better before.

Psychologists call this the halo effect—creating an idealized or critical view of something based on your initial impression. "Coined by psychologist Edward Thorndike, the Halo Effect describes people's tendency to let one positive trait guide their total opinion of a person, product, or experience," says behavior-change strategist Jennifer Clinehens. "Thorndike discovered the effect after noticing that commanding officers in the military judged their soldiers to be either all good or all bad. Almost no one was described as good at one thing but bad at another. One positive or negative trait disproportionately influenced the officers' opinions."

For instance, if you have ice cream for the first time ever at your neighborhood corner store, then that first experience of the sweet, cold, and sticky sensation raises your view of the product. I know that the cheesesteak, specifically from the bodega down the street from my late grandmother, is the best sandwich in the world. Seriously, you couldn't get a better one in Camden, New Jersey, or even in the tri-state. Trust me, I've tried! I can taste it right now. But that simple sub with meat, provolone cheese, and grilled onions ties directly to my childhood: playing with my favorite cousins, my older relatives sneaking me candy, getting hugs from all the aunties. I can think of a dozen other foods that give me that same reaction, as I'm sure you can too. And I know other Jerseyites are making an equally passionate argument for their corner cheesesteaks. Most of us recognize our biases in food, music, and other specific cultural experiences. When it comes to our other firsts, though—our first management position, our first job where we bonded with our co-workers beyond the workplace, our first role making enough money to feel financially secure—then it is a lot tougher to see our idealization.

Our bias ties into a new phenomenon, too, called "nostalgic preferences." In short, the past will always be better than the present. It doesn't matter if it was your first time or not. "Memory seems to operate much like a record store, stocking the hits of the past, and both the hits and the duds of the present," says Carnegie Mellon University associate professor of marketing and Tepper School of Business BP Junior Faculty Chair, Carey K. Morewedge. "Rather than recognize this bias, however, we mistakenly believe that what we remember is representative of the entire category of experiences, giving rise to nostalgic preferences."

You may see the problem now. You hate your current role and pine for the position you had before. So you quit or are let go. You then convince yourself that the job you just left wasn't that bad. The damage is threefold: you frame the narrative so idealistically that you don't break down exactly why you were so unhappy; you don't honor those intense feelings in the past and thus set yourself up with some serious emotional baggage to unpack in your next job; and, since you didn't learn and crystallize the lessons from the past, you are more likely to be in a similar situation again with any new role you take. Like any breakup, you need time to mourn the loss, reflect on what you'll miss, and then synthesize any insights. If you're like me, you may have even found yourself angry at being at a job, sad when the job ended, and missing it much later. We are all guilty of a little revisionist history.

Unfortunately, our myopic past-idealizing approach makes us brittle and harsh in how we treat ourselves and, worse, each other. *Rising Strong* author Brené Brown calls this "gold-plated grit." I remember going through a personal loss and sharing it with a loved one. "I'm sorry," they said—and then, without missing a beat, said, "Just let it go and move on." *That* is the impact of gold-plated grit: "I respect that you're going through a shitty experience, and I believe in my heart that I can relate or even have gone through something I consider similar. I dealt with it by not fully dealing with it. See! I'm fine! And you're fine too. *I said* you're fine too." A key tell of gold-plated grit is seeing whoever is slinging it become uncomfortable with your vulnerability. It also shows you how vulnerable *they* feel about their own unresolved experiences.

As Brown says in *Rising Strong: How the Ability to Reset Transforms the Way We Live, Love, Parent, and Lead*:

> Embracing failure without acknowledging the real hurt and fear that it can cause, or the complex journey that underlies rising strong, is gold-plating grit. To strip failure of its real emotional consequences is to scrub the concepts of grit and resilience of the very qualities that make them both so important—toughness, doggedness, and perseverance.

All this matters because your new normal cannot be based on an idealized past. It is like wishing for a return to the *Leave It to Beaver* era without acknowledging the negroes being fire-hosed by racist cops right down the street, or pining for the lack of responsibility in your childhood and conveniently ignoring the virtually complete lack of agency you had in your life. There is more racial equity here in America compared to the fifties, just as you have more control over your life now than you did as a young dependent. When we're fixated on what *was*, all our progress is shunned, ignored, or taken for granted. We don't honor how far we've come; therefore, we don't honor ourselves. So how can we expect our next employer, business partner, or investor to recognize our value more than our past experiences when we don't even see our own worth?

"Every interaction is a building block, and you're either adding or subtracting to this foundation to get closer to your true self and, therefore, your true worth," I say in *Bring Your Worth: Level Up Your Creative Power, Value & Service to the World*. "As many wise people have said, setbacks are not failures, but information: data on what you are not, figures showing your real path, live feedback on your pain points. The times when you undervalue yourself—and actually get what you asked for!—are just as valuable as the times you are able to reflect your true worth. It all depends on what you do with the insight."

What you can do is use your past neither as a beautiful, unreachable beacon nor as a dark, evil moment in your life. You can use it as an observation. This boss made me feel small whenever we worked together. Why? I built such a strong relationship with my co-workers, and I miss them more than the job itself. How did I connect with them so much, in ways that I never did at any other job, and how can I show up that way again in my next career move? The pay I was getting did not make the job worthwhile. Where did the gap between my worth and my work come from? And is there a way I can decrease the gap next time around?

Data doesn't mean putting your feelings into a box. If anything, it is the opposite. Before you remix your career *now*, you absolutely have to understand what you felt *then*. The honesty helps you see that few of your jobs were extremely good or bad and—perhaps the most difficult, important realization—that you played a role in your experiences in those same jobs. *If you don't acknowledge your part in your own career, then you are giving away your power.* Making your happiness dependent on getting the next right job minimizes your joy now and pushes away your chances of finding your best position later.

As Brené Brown says in *Rising Strong*:

> While vulnerability is the birthplace of many of the fulfilling experiences we long for—love, belonging, joy, creativity, and trust, to name a few—the process of regaining our emotional footing in the midst of struggle is where our courage is tested and our values are forged. Rising strong after a fall is how we cultivate wholeheartedness in our lives; it's the process that teaches us the most about who we are.

Look back to move forward.

CHAPTER 1.

MAKE YOUR OWN
METRICS FOR SUCCESS

A s a business coach, I get asked common questions such as how to make room for your new business vision. You don't like where you are, or, at a minimum, you picture someplace better to be. You will be better once you get there. The messy middle, transforming from one career to the next, is where we tend to get too intimidated to fully move forward.

We often don't successfully change, because we haven't made space for the new life to begin. It's like developing a new area of your proverbial house. First, you have to figure out why the current situation isn't working. The time, energy, and other resources required to make the new thing should not only be worth the effort but also worth the opportunity, cost, and resources required to start something new rather than keeping things the same. Then, you have to get rid of what you've got. This is where many of us get stuck. This is where we get scared. This is the part we envision before we even start that prevents us from starting at all.

To use an analogy, we are constantly between the shore and the island. The shore on which you sit is what you already know: the safety, however uncomfortable, of what you have now. The island that you can't see is what you intuitively know: the vision for doing your true work, making your best impact, and earning your true worth in your career. You know it's out there, though you may have been convinced otherwise. You recognize that it is available, even as those around you may think your ambition is folly. Each and every one of us knows when we are in what *The Big Leap* author Gay Hendricks calls our zone of genius, that place where we work and enter what author Mihaly Csikszentmihalyi calls flow. It is where we feel at home. And we know on the shore ain't it.

In *The Big Leap*, Gay Hendricks breaks down four zones we all inhabit: the zone of incompetence, the zone of competence, the zone of excellence, and the zone of genius. In the zone of incompetence, we are doing something we are not skilled in. In the zone of competence, we are doing something efficiently, but realize that others are just as efficient and our skill set is average. In the zone of excellence, we are doing something with very high skill, usually based on our own dedication. Lastly, in the zone of genius, we are doing something that is natural, if not innate. In my interpretation, the zone of genius cannot be taught, only revealed. Your zone of genius is yours and yours alone. However, you have to *own* it.

"The temptation is strong to remain in the Zone of Excellence; it's where your own addiction to comfort wants you to stay," Hendricks writes in *The Big Leap*. "It's also where your family, friends, and organization want you to stay. You're reliable there, and you provide a steady supply of all the things that family, friends, and organizations thrive on. The problem is that a deep, sacred part of you will wither and die if you stay inside your Zone of Excellence."

For me, my zone of excellence is journalism: three decades in the field, master's in Magazine Publishing, thousands of high-profile articles published. I also remember the moment when I launched my first startup, took "journalist" off my business card, and shared with my wife that being only a freelance writer and author wasn't it anymore. There would be some ups and downs, but I knew I couldn't continue on the path I was on and make the impact I was meant to make. There was more for me to do beyond my journalism career thus far.

My zone of genius is guiding non-traditional entrepreneurs: inspiring the next generation of side hustlers, solopreneurs, and those who don't fit in the straight white male Ivy League college dropout Silicon Valley founder stereotype. There is no competition. And the more I learn, serve, and build the community, the deeper I tap into that unique zone of genius.

What gets me excited is that my confidence doesn't come from ego: it comes from owning my story. And I feel comfortable shining even brighter because I know you have your own story too.

But you gotta leave the shore to get it.

In an interview with *Forbes*, Hendricks says:

Most successful people are operating in their zone of excellence, in which they are doing things at which they are highly skilled. This zone is ultimately unsatisfying, though, because it does not engage the innate genius of the individual. As with any other kind of lasting, meaningful change, commitment is the gateway to the zone of genius. When I work with busy executives, I start by asking them to make a commitment to blocking out just ten minutes a day in their calendars to devote to cultivating their genius. The ten minutes can involve journaling, meditating or any number of other activities, just as long as you are focusing on your genius for ten uninterrupted minutes. After you have gotten your ten minutes a day in your routine, then bump it up to fifteen minutes. Ultimately I want to see people I work with spending 90 percent of their time in their zone of genius, but you've got to start somewhere and my recommendation is to start with ten minutes a day.

It takes a minute to sink in. The stuff you are good at (your zone of excellence) is your comfort zone. It is the shore, though it may not feel like it. That's the danger. The stuff you feel most alive in (your zone of genius) is *out there*. It is so original that you have to take a risk to fully show it. If you got immediate acceptance, then your view wouldn't be original to you. Your zone of genius isn't meant to be a shared experience.

We get stuck in the in-between, that place when we're swimming and don't physically see the island yet but also can no longer see the shore we've left behind. We feel adrift. And with no metrics and no landmarks on the horizon, we don't have any way of knowing whether we are making progress, whether we are coming or going. We feel like we're running in place. We feel like we're wasting our time. So we panic, hustling to get back to the shore we left, back to the devil we know, burning precious energy in our erratic movements and, perhaps unconsciously, hoping to shrink back into the box we outgrew. When we make it back to shore, we'll be sure to share the message of dangers, of growing too much, of how we should be happy with the crumbs of our worth. How many times has someone—a teacher, a colleague, a loved one—shat on your ambition, your ideas, your vision, seemingly unprovoked? I love storytelling, and I love hearing other people's stories, and journalism has given me the power and the privilege to ask people, essentially, "What happened?" I will tell you what happened: that teacher, that colleague, that loved one came back to the shore. That's not enough, though. They feel like their job is to warn the next potential Icarus of the dangers of flying too close to the sun. But, as Seth Godin once said, they seem to forget about the risk of the Greek hero coming too close to the water below and drowning from his own fear of flight.

Lastly, when we do commit to the in-between, we can begin furnishing our new structure. It's crucial to create metrics, landmarks, and intentions not only to survive the uncomfortable limbo but also to build our next venture in a way that makes navigating that limbo worthwhile. This intentionality is critical. It is that moment when I'm with a coaching client and they are explaining the problems they are having with their work environment, why their co-founder relationship has gone south, or where the roadblock they are hitting with their newest creative project seems to have come from. And they talk about the previous work environment, the last startup relationship, or the preceding project—and realize that they can replace the names and tell the exact same story. Their eyes light up. Oh, I swam to another island and built the same darn structure. To paraphrase an old saying, if you start your day and run into an asshole, then you ran into an asshole; but if you start your day and you run into more than one asshole, then *you* are the asshole.

Don't be the asshole. You deserve better.

The trifecta of letting go of what you've got, sitting in the in-between, and intentionally building your next act comes down to three steps.

The first step is making room for your next act, and that means saying no. A lot. Unfortunately, saying yes to everything means eventually saying no to other things. As I share in *Build From Now: How to Know Your Power, See Your Abundance & Nourish the World*, we have four primary resources: Focus, Agility, Time, and Energy. They aren't infinite, and, depending on where you are in your life, some of these are ridiculously scarce. We tend to fall apart when we believe we can have and do it all, thinking we can stay on the shore while we reach the island or even going after multiple islands at once and scattering our precious resources. Having an abundance mindset will get you far, but this is one of the few times when Carol Dweck's lamented "scarcity mindset" actually comes in handy: you can't just *make* more time, nor can you just make more energy. They will come from something else. You may as well make that a conscious process.

Depending on where you are in your career, what to say no to may feel obvious. For instance, it could be refusing to start your next book idea in earnest before you get a rough draft done of the current one, or simply committing to turning off the TV for an hour every night to research your next business opportunity. Sometimes simple measures have the greatest effect. However, this mindset is just as powerful in subtle ways. "No" could mean delegating a project at your job so you can put more brain power into your next act; or doing what corporate coach Whitney Johnson calls a "slingshot" move, taking or staying in a lower hierarchical position so you can do the work and research necessary to propel yourself even farther than you would otherwise.

Saying no more often actually gives you more space for your next thing. You just need to be comfortable with creating a void. There are many thoughtful, honest ways to say no. And it's even easier to say it when you are going toward your career goal with clarity and confidence:

1. "When we work together, I want to make sure you have my full attention": One of my biggest pet peeves is when a business partner commits to working together but obviously has too much on his plate. The problem is that I do my best to make sure that I'm not overextended so he gets the attention and details deserved—and I assume others do the same.

2. "I need to respect those to whom I've already committed": It reminds me of the adage "If someone gossips to you about other people, you can bet they are gossiping about you to other people." The same could be said for other business dealings: People who are unwilling to say no to you, even though they know they can't give you quality time, are the same people who will willingly sacrifice their commitment to you to work with someone else to whom they can't say no.

A potential collaborator may not like that you are prioritizing others' previous needs over their current needs, but they should respect it. If they don't respect your commitment to others, then that often reflects their own principles—and it may be a warning sign to keep in the back of your mind.

3. "We should make sure the timing is good": Your business should naturally evolve, whether this means changing your product scope or identifying a new customer base. It means yesterday's great projects are today's misfires and last year's potential partnerships are now pretty lukewarm.

There are amazing collaborators, clients, and mentors I would love to work with right now; but as I focus in on my core business, I've had to gently let them know that our time to work together isn't here . . . yet. This leaves the door open for later opportunities and also confirms that you respect other people's time and are keen not to waste it.

The second step is respecting the uncomfortable in-between, and that means holding a space for what will be. It doesn't matter if you hate your job, can't stand your co-workers, or complain endlessly about your organization. It is still familiar to you; and even if you don't consciously get more out of your job than a paycheck, you still have become accustomed to that stream of routines, structures, and security. We are, after all, creatures of habit.

In his book *The Power of Habit*, Charles Duhigg shows research saying that it is sometimes easier to replace one routine with another one than just going cold turkey. It may be harder to leave a work situation if your social group is there, so the transition may be meeting with those friends after work instead of during lunch, or cultivating another social group more closely aligned with where you want to go next. Or, perhaps, you commit to reading about or listening to information about your next act on the morning commute, easing the way toward spending even more time with your future venture later.

The best habit you can cultivate to navigate the messy middle is service. Serving others has a bad rap—no one wants to be subservient to their boss or be treated poorly because "the customer is always right." That's not what I mean—nor do, I believe, the many leaders who came before me. Serving means identifying the community you want to support, figuring out from what they need what you can provide, and delivering it to them as consistently as possible at the highest feasible level. The latter is the crucial part, but it's worth discussing the first two aims.

Identifying the community you want to support requires your doing research on whom you want to impact before you go after that job interview, create that product, or launch that side hustle. Are there people in your circle who represent your ideal customer or the target of the organization you want to join? Where are these people, online or otherwise? It doesn't have to be a deep recon. You just want to get to know the community you want to impact; and in getting to know them, you can better see where their gaps and pain points may be.

"Knowing the audience, spending months scouring the groundwork and doing reconnaissance like the military. Always start with a deep connection," says *The 48 Laws of Power* author Robert Greene. He adds that the difference between businesses that do the work of listening to their customers and those that don't is obvious. "I gave a talk for Microsoft and got to know the people, and the problem was that the great creative developers started in the Microsoft bubble and had no connection to what people really needed. With Google[,] on the other hand, they kept their feet on the ground, observing what the audience and their customers needed as a starting point."

And in connecting as much as possible with your audience, you will have an easier time determining what they need from what you can provide. My one-on-one coaching practice has been a wonderful career development, a personally fulfilling cause, and a nice income stream, but I had no intention of becoming such a coach. In fact, if you had asked me a decade ago, I would have told you I was happy writing books and doing an occasional speaking gig to promote them. But then I came up with a startup idea, So Quotable, and launched the app while being the primary caregiver of the son of my partner and myself, which led to my first TED Talk, an even more popular and profitable startup, Cuddlr, and doing a best-selling book, *The Bite-Sized Entrepreneur*, about the entire experience. The book put me on the road, and attendees would come up after the speaking engagements to ask questions. One of the most common ones was something like "Hey, do you want to grab a drink to talk more?" I'd be somewhere between embarrassed, as I wasn't sure if they were asking me out, and confused, as I literally wrote a book that answers all your questions. We don't need to talk more! Luckily, my dense perception finally recognized what was happening: the book obviously didn't answer all their questions, and the knowledge they wanted was specific and nuanced.

They wanted a coach.

The next time someone asked, I responded much more open-mindedly. And I got my first of many clients.

Sometimes your naïveté about your next move can be your biggest advantage. In my case, I had no interest in becoming a coach—which meant that all the signals that pointed to people needing me to do coaching were genuine. There was no ego involved. This is how they were asking me to show up. I didn't have to worry about the dark side of knowing what I wanted to do before I knew what my community needed. It's like the person who always knew what they wanted to do. You may have wanted to be a world-famous singer since you were a little girl, but what if you can't hold a pitch or don't have the lungs to carry a serious tune? It's not a matter of saying you can't do it. It's actually quite the opposite: you may be able to do it, but desire may take precedence over practicality. You may be too wrapped up in your dream to hear—quite literally!—that you are delivering flat notes. And buoyed by that desire, your myopic goal could blind you— and your ego could block you—from admitting that you need to improve in specific areas, which, ironically, might stop you from actually reaching your goal. It is why prodigies often burn out by adulthood, as it is hard to hear where you need to grow over the sound of unending praise from yourself and others. My previous pivot into public speaking happened when I was asked to speak at TED. I had had speech therapy around kindergarten, when I was the age of my youngest son now, to work through an impediment, and spent years being frustrated that I seemingly wasn't able to communicate the big ideas in my head as easily as other people. A big reason why I've had success now as a professional public speaker is because I see clearly where my flaws lie, how I can improve, and what I need to deliver to help my audience the most. Take heart if you're not exactly sure how you want to serve your community, as you can then be more receptive to what exactly they need. In short, success comes when it is not about you.

"Many of our fears are based on the workings of the ego, the part of us that's focused on getting recognition and protecting us from social ostracism. In the Zone of Genius, your ego is unnecessary; living there is its own reward," Gay Hendricks writes in *The Big Leap.* "In the Zone of Genius, you cease to care about recognition or ostracism. Once you make a commitment to inhabiting your full potential, your ego is suddenly faced with extinction."

The beauty is that the selfless act of delivering to them as consistently as possible at the highest feasible level—the last element to navigating the career in-between—automatically creates security for you. Instead of the common capricious metrics of annual salary, hours per week, and corporate titles, you are focused on the cycle of serving. You create something for whom you serve, you give something to whom you serve, and then you revise what you serve based on their feedback and evolving needs. What you create could be a new conversation or a new product or service. What you give them can be your attention or your time. What you get in return could be a "no," a subtle nod of the head, or their spreading what you're doing—and why they should get involved—to others in the community. That's why it is so crucial that you know what is needed by the person or people you serve *before* you decide to bestow something on them. When launching something new, *Side Hustle* author Chris Guillebeau has a simple, great strategy: Sell, Create, Ship. Sounds out of chronological order, doesn't it? It's not. We have bought into a different rubric: Create, Ship, Sell. The prevailing myth, particularly in the traditionally creative fields, is to build something in your proverbial basement or on your kitchen table, make sure it is perfect, and then give it to the intended audience. This is often a recipe for heartbreak. I know, because my heart has been broken many times too. In the context of service, you can probably see the issue. When you create something in isolation—whether with a great idea you have in your head that you don't share with others for feedback, or by spending years working on a project with no insight from others—then it becomes less likely that you are going to make an impact and more likely that you will waste your time. Guillebeau's approach for, say, launching a new online course would be to first offer the upcoming course to the community (*Sell*). Then, if people are interested, to develop the course (*Create*). And only lastly, to share the completed course with the community (*Ship*).

This approach gives us exponential power and fortitude. You know that the community wants it—because they've told you! So much of our creative, entrepreneurial, and corporate anxiety comes from our not knowing if our idea or purpose will be what our community needs. Sure, we want to know we've done well. But that need for reassurance can turn into needing to be validated, not just in the genius of our idea, but in our existence and our worth. And suddenly you're swimming between that shore and that island, panicking because you now are not so sure about your purpose. Validation is a sneaky, insidious concept, disguised as security: "I'm not going to pursue this idea unless I know it will be profitable"; "I will move forward once I know no one will disagree with my theory"; "I can't wait to share this book, but only if it will be a best seller." We're less likely to ship. In the slim chance that we do ship, then we could be devastated that the feedback didn't match this obscure metric that was, ultimately, out of our control. And, before we know it, we are scurrying back to the proverbial shore. By going to the community first, as I did with being asked to coach or with TED asking me to speak, then some of that validity-hinged anxiety goes away. You then focus on what Seth Godin's recent book calls *The Practice*, the act of showing up consistently for whom you serve. They say what they want, you deliver what they want, and then they pay you—in money, in attention, in trust—enabling you to do it again. Then again. Then again.

Service is infinite. So, then, is your ability to go from shore to island. You don't need to rush, because you're standing in the space you are looking to become your next home. Better yet, you are priming the pump for future success. My serving my audience to the highest of my ability—writing honest, practical books—got them ready to receive me on a bigger, more intimate level—as a one-on-one coach. But if I hadn't focused on serving them, then that path would not have opened, while they also wouldn't have recognized my value at a higher, bigger price point. My coaching currently costs a customer twenty times the price of one of my books. They wouldn't be as eager, let alone willing, to invest in their future; and in my business, they wouldn't be looking to pay for my higher services if they didn't see me bring my worth in my books on a much less risky level.

I was holding a space for my next act and didn't even know it. This is why you need to focus not on the money or the clout or the title, but on the service. By shifting to your community's needs, you could already be laying the foundation for your career—and your future success.

➡

CHAPTER 2.

DESIGN YOUR LIFE AROUND YOUR CAREER, NOT VICE VERSA

I became an entrepreneur at the same time I became the primary caregiver of my four-month-old. It was a time full of discovery—and, initially, of frustration. Progress on my business seemed to take forever, especially since I was waking up at 3:15 a.m. to do work before my son awoke. Then I had a moment of clarity: I needed to stretch my timeline. As a new stay-at-home dad, it would take me two months to do what a young, single entrepreneur could do in two weeks. I would succeed; it would just take longer. Six months after starting, I launched my first app and, from the exposure, did my first TED Talk too. Your frustration may not be in whether or not you can do it, but *if you can do it within your ideal timeline.*

For example, if you have an average American salary and want to be a millionaire within the next year, then some extraordinary pressures come into play. Are you going to win the lottery? Take the cash you've got and invest in something risky with a potentially high return? Or will you bend your ethics or allow yourself to be treated poorly by powerful people promising quick riches? The dynamics change, though, when you want to be a millionaire in a decade. The math becomes less brutal. Your opportunities expand. And you have to come up with something more sustainable.

It also brings up something we often forget in our ambitious pursuits: quality of life. I lived in Silicon Valley during one of the gold-rush eras— from 2008 to 2011. Many billion-dollar companies, called unicorns, were started at that time. Steve Jobs was still active and influential, up until his death which, in retrospect, marked the end of that era. And young, eager men came to the Bay Area to discover the next hot idea, get their startup up and out as soon as possible, and hope to be acquired by one of the five big guys (FAANG, which is an acronym for Facebook, Amazon, Apple, Netflix, and Google). To paraphrase one founder I knew, the goal was to do all-nighters until the product shipped, get tens of millions of dollars from one of the FAANG, and buy an island somewhere on which to retire early. This, of course, didn't happen to him or virtually any of the other hope-fuls wide-eyed and hopping off the proverbial bus like a farmboy arriving on L.A.'s Skid Row. The ones I knew would have an idea that was inoffen-sive, but not too much different from that of their peers, spend a week or a month burning the candle at both ends, and then ship out a mediocre product and begin pursuing their next potential lottery ticket. They were the lucky ones. In most cases, they would burn out and either head back to their hometown or still hang out in Silicon Valley as a remote, distant ver-sion of their previous selves. The saddest part was that most of them were in their early twenties. Just turning thirty at the time, I realized how much time they had and, in a cruel irony of the young, how they felt like they had no time at all. Tomorrow didn't exist to them, so they pushed themselves so hard that they didn't create a tomorrow for themselves at all.

What the dream of going hard, selling your company, and then rest-ing misses is twofold. First, whatever you pursue is likely going to take longer than you plan for, but, because you believe it will be a quick turn-around, you are willing to make bigger sacrifices. Skipping meals and doing 48-hour days is, frankly, sometimes part of brutal deadlines (I'm all too familiar as a former newspaper journalist and a two-time startup founder). In the tech world, we call this "crunch time." As in, a specific time when we are going to crunch. Then you celebrate the success and go pass out to rest for a while. But it is called crunch *time*, not crunch *life*. Those extreme circumstances are special to the moment, not meant to be a fixed standard of living. Overoptimism poisons the well: you believe your success is right around the corner, so you compromise your health and balance in ways that are suitable for short-term success but never bother to update your ideas based on new data and circumstances. Ironically, the crunch-time mentality makes you too busy to reconsider your lifestyle and too myopic to notice the toll it is taking on your soul. Second, that rest life isn't realistic, because you would have been living the opposite lifestyle weeks, months, years, or even decades before your victory. It is why seniors are more likely to have major health issues immediately after they do retire: not only do some underestimate the structure that work gives in their lives but they also may have a jarring reframing of their purpose. What if you do sell your company and can spend your days on your own private island? That's not a purpose: that's a goal. And countless founders who have actually achieved these rare successes find themselves lost after their win.

"So with well over half his life ahead of him, the man who created an entire universe, whose persona was synonymous with it and who received the wrath of his community for abandoning it, must now figure out exactly who he is," *Forbes* magazine wrote about the 35-year-old Markus Persson, who co-founded the game Minecraft and sold it, with his majority stake, to Microsoft for $2.7 billion. "The results so far are unimpressive, as he's mostly acted like a dog chasing cars. When Persson decided to buy a house in Beverly Hills, he went for a $70 million, 23,000-square-foot mega-mansion, the most expensive home ever in an enclave known for them. He's become known for spending upward of $180,000 a night at Las Vegas nightclubs. He and Mojang cofounder Jakob Porsér have started a company called Rubberbrain in case they think of a new game idea—but right now he can't focus much on any."

Not one game has shipped yet. It's been more than a decade.

This reminds me of a classic fisherman's tale. While vacationing on a Mexican beach, a posh businessman watches an older gentleman leisurely take a boat out to sea, catch live seafood, and prepare it for him. It was the best fish he had ever had. "This is extraordinary!" he says. "Other people need to know about this. You only have this one little boat? I want to invest."

"Thanks, sir, but I love my life now. I live on the beach. Fish all day. Work at my own pace. I have everything I need."

"But imagine: having a whole fleet of boats working for you. It would be hard work to train them, but once you do, the money will be rolling in fast!"

"Then what?"

"Well, then we could use the capital to expand even more! Not just this beach, but this whole shoreline as far as your eyes can see!"

"And then?"

"Then your name will have enough clout to be licensed on products so you'd have all this additional income coming in!"

"And then what, sir?"

"And then," he says, winded from his own excitement, "you can live on the beach, fish as much as you want, and work only when you want to."

It is so important to know what you value now. You may not be as far off as you think. But not knowing your values can take you much farther off course.

"People tend to start with a business model and then become unhappy when their days are filled with tasks they don't enjoy," Paul Jarvis says in *Company of One*. "Instead of thinking, What product can I create? or What service can I offer?, [*Atomic Habits* author James Clear] believes that we should first think: What type of life do I want? And how do I want to spend my days? Then you can work backward from there into a business model that allows you to create scalable systems to deliver your product to your audience."

The solution is to figure out your optimum outcome—again, having a vision for the career you want—and then to work beginning with the end in mind.

The end, though, shouldn't be based on some metric outside of your control. In the past decade, I realized I didn't want to spend all my time trading time for money. Journalists like myself are trained to focus on one story, write the story, and then move on to the next story. After all, today's newspaper will be replaced by another on the newsstand tomorrow. We get paid a flat rate or salary for our work. No royalties involved. It's not dissimilar to the average nine-to-five. You agree to a fixed compensation, an organization gives it to you consistently, and you get the same financial result no matter how you contribute to the overall profits. The real gift a steady job gives you isn't money, but security. You know where your next meal is coming from. The benefit? Your financial station in life is fixed. The tradeoff? Your financial station in life is *fixed*.

And after a decade-plus as a full-time freelance writer, I realized where my road was leading: to more of the same. I wanted the freedom that comes from money coming in while I enjoy my life. I started a column with *Inc.* magazine that pays me money per view for articles I write once. I launched an independent book, *The Bite-Sized Entrepreneur*, and it became a best seller and turned into my indie imprint, Bring Your Worth, that pays me money per item sold for books I write once. And I created an online, self-guided boot camp to help people do their side hustles, which pays me money per student for a curriculum I designed once. I have more than fifty passive income streams as of this writing.

Most importantly, all these decisions as well as the desired outcome were under my control.

Using metrics outside of your control has three major issues: vulnerability to outside factors, diminished power from a capricious community, and potential loss of self-purpose. Banking on a best seller means trusting you'll have the right idea, written in a certain way, at a precise time in the market. Needing constant adoration from whom you serve means you may provide them with what they want, but not necessarily what they need. Using the public as your personal north star means you flip-flop with the winds of change, losing your unique voice in the process. In my case, multiplying my passive income means I don't need to have another best seller to bring in steady income. I can create work that can be respected later rather than having an immediate resonance, and I have higher consistency because what I deliver is based on a steady standard. Picture a neighborhood storefront that was a Chinese restaurant a minute ago, then a hardware store, and now a jewelry spot. What are the chances that you'll go inside to check it out, let alone that you'll become a regular there? We don't trust that it'll be around very long.

My passive income streams can vary from pennies to thousands of dollars, depending on the needs and interests of my community. However, I had to first forgo the big, onetime article bucks to get the long-term, slower column money, the upfront money and safety of a traditionally published book, and the security of teaching a class within a classic educational structure.

We can all do this. The dual challenge is letting go of the guaranteed route and cultivating the patience to see small, slow results over time. In *The Passive Writer: 5 Steps to Earning Money in Your Sleep*, Jeanette Hurt and I share the dilemma that independents and even traditionally employed folks have: "The most powerful passive income opportunities *will* take time, but we often don't take the time to do it. . . . The sacrifice can feel too great to plan for the next year's rewards, let alone the next quarter. The beauty is we are actually giving space for future success."

The plan is to sacrifice comfort now for a better flow later.

We'll talk more about this in chapter 18, Understanding Passive Income and Other Opportunities Available to All.

One of the biggest blocks to having the career you want is focusing on *looking* the part rather than *being* the part. Early in my career, I met ambitious entrepreneurs who printed pristine business cards, bought expensive website domain names, and talked loudly about their intentions and future sales. The emphasis was heavy on future, though, as they didn't have a lick of product. They didn't even have a prototype or a test audience to give it to. As we say today, they want the clout before the work.

I share as much in *The Ultimate Bite-Sized Entrepreneur*:

> It is tweeting about the next novel you are going to do when you haven't written the last five books you've talked about. It is launching a Kickstarter campaign for something you know you don't have the passion to follow through on. It is networking at conferences, at parties, and at coffeeshops about your brilliant idea that you could have—should have—started literally years ago. It is the flash before the fire, the dessert before the main course. It is cheating. We worry about selling out for security or big bucks, but the most dangerous selling out is you removing the work and soaking in the fun and the accolades that are supposed to be a reward for that very work. There is mounting scientific proof that saying you are going to do something and getting props for it taps the same part of your brain that recognizes reward for actually doing it. In other words, you could lose the motivation to achieve your goal simply because you've already gotten part of the reward: Recognition.

This is why you need to determine the life you want to have and then move toward molding your best career. How can you know your next best move if you don't know where you want to end up?

"We're sold a bill of goods from society: 'If your business doesn't look a certain way, you're not successful,'" entrepreneur coach and *Everything Is Figureoutable* author Marie Forleo told me. "You have to define success on your own terms. To me, success means liking who I am, what I am, and how I do it."

This powerful argument is worth breaking down. Liking who you are, what you are, and how you do it means having peace with whatever role you play in the world. It informs your career decisions: you'll think twice before accepting an opportunity that doesn't fit your personal ethics. You'll take more pride in your worth, because it not only reflects a financial reward but an emotional benefit too. And you'll create more opportunities, because the clearer your vision for the impact you want to make, the more people will recognize a kindred bond with you and want to help your cause.

There's an even stronger reason why we should heed Forleo's advice: the more successful you become, the less agency you have over the opportunities that come through your door. It's why artists, creators, and business-folks initially seem so focused, so righteous, so *pure*. The money isn't there yet, so they have to be committed because of what they are contributing, not what they are getting. The prestige hasn't arrived, as no one knows who the hell they are yet, so they are showing up for the practice of art itself. And the public hasn't christened their best work yet, so there is no pressure of impostor syndrome or previous standard that they have to fight against when they create. They are free.

As a former DJ and music critic, I have always marveled at the first-album/book/creation curse. An artist or group's initial outing is raw, uncut, and direct. They are not catering to the masses, as they are too naïve to do so even if they want to! They are not living up to the ghost of previous work, as they are an unknown quantity, maybe even to themselves. And they finally have the opportunity to tell their story in a complete manner. It is why we call the second outing the "sophomore jinx," as it is way too easy to overthink what went right and wrong with the first one. As we used to say, the second album has a year or two of thought. The first album represented their entire prior life.

I experienced this when my startup, Cuddlr, became the number one Apple app in 2014 and was acquired less than a year later. As I share in *Build From Now*, I felt this quiet personal expectation to do it over again—even though no one expected as much:

> There is something unusual about the air on the mountaintop. I've felt lost twice in my life: The year escaping Hurricane Katrina and the year after selling my second startup, Cuddlr. In both cases, my identity—as a Crescent City resident or as a co-founder—and a home—New Orleans or with the Cuddlr community we cultivated—were suddenly gone. It didn't matter if one was by force and the other was by choice. And while I recognize now that the months following Katrina held me in a low-grade PTSD, our sale of Cuddlr showed me how much I identified with the 3:15 a.m. business meetings, constant limelight from the *New York Times*, *WSJ*, and other outlets, and the potential of more growth, more community, more opportunities. Suddenly, the light switch turned off. I was no longer a founder. I was just a writer. And perhaps I'd never create again.
>
> Being famous or prolific won't help you succeed again. What matters is the work and your intention. Is your product or service being done with the audience at the forefront? Are you contributing something more to the cultural conversation? Ego-driven enterprises rarely rise as high as purely-motivated work—and we are in the most danger of doing the former after a big win.

As we gain the money, prestige, and expectations, then the opportunities available begin to multiply. Partners want to be associated with your name brand, like hiring you as a consultant or courting you to join their organization. Your reputation precedes you. And, in the ultimate contradiction, you have more choices than ever but may be less likely to take a risk because you have more to defend.

Your best opportunity to design your best career may be right now, before you become known for your gift, get your worth in the marketplace, and create a standard that you feel pressure to uphold. It's not about reinvention *per se*—no matter where you go, there you are—but about leaning into the future you are creating for yourself, the community you want to serve, and, ultimately, the world.

→

CHAPTER 3.

SET YOUR LIFE GOALS

*E*verything Is Figureoutable author Marie Forleo has had more odd jobs than a Hollywood actor with a script. She has been an MTV-featured hip-hop dance instructor, a mover and shaker on the Wall Street floor, a cheerleader, a bartender, and more. What's fascinating isn't the variety, but the lack of shame in her winding path to creating her coaching empire. In fact, her tone implies a direct lineage between the side hustles and the success.

"For those seven years of hustling, that was by choice! I loved aspects of it: loved dancing, loved bartending to connect with people. It takes a lot of courage and strength to say, 'I'm doing exactly what I'm doing to take care of my family and I'm going to enjoy it,'" she told me. "It will transform throughout your lifetime."

And she adds, "To feel shameful is a recipe for failure. You're doing the work you need to do, but not giving yourself permission to feel joy for showing up."

According to emotional-intelligence pioneer Brené Brown, guilt is when you fall short of your own expectations, while shame is when you feel like you fall short of others' expectations. The real failure in your career isn't in taking on a variety of roles, taking the scenic route toward your ultimate goal, or leaning on a day job to fund your dream: it is wallowing in shame around your choices, based on how you think others will judge you.

The problem, as Forleo says, is that you're going to be doing the work anyway! There are three big ideas as you think about what kind of career you want around the contour of your life: success doesn't mean happiness; your career is different from your job; and desires will change.

Success is relative, but it never guarantees that you'll be happy. This seems obvious, doesn't it? But consciously or unconsciously, we lean toward making life goals contingent on the next thing. You will always need more resources than you have, more time than you've got, and more energy than you can muster. My two dozen books, TED Talks, and even my last acquired startup were all done under some kind of resource poverty: time, money, or location. And, believe it or not, those actually made the opportunities not only better but also increased the chances that those opportunities would actually show up. On time scarcity, isn't it amazing how we manage to get our projects done just in the nick of time, no matter how long the deadline? We always pace ourselves, expanding and contracting our productivity, based on the time available. Our biggest constraints are often personal: relationship needs like our families, physical needs like our rest, or emotional needs like our hobbies. *It's not about time, though, but efficiency.* On financial scarcity, we may dream about being billionaires, but complete financial freedom can actually be a detriment to productivity. Artists and entrepreneurs often thrive when they have fewer resources simply because they must be more creative and innovative. *Waiting until your money is better is often a mistake.* And on location scarcity, it's not about being in the perfect city—especially post-COVID. I have lived all across America and experienced business opportunities in the Midwest, down South, and on either coast. I also know entrepreneurs and businesspeople who are sitting on their laurels until they can move to a major city, which is akin to an author waiting to type any words until they meet an agent. The question is, *where can you make the most impact?*

On St. Patrick's Day 2020, as America began sheltering in place, professional speakers like myself faced a tough choice: learn to do virtual talks from home or wait things out until we could safely do in-person talks again. Of course, most of us had begun public speaking in the first place *because* we liked to be on stage connecting with a large audience. The decision was tough, because we didn't know when COVID-19 would be even a little bit under control—scientists, governments, and other authorities were saying anywhere from summer 2020 to, well, never. Worse, there were no vaccines on the horizon. We had to decide. Well, we didn't have to decide: some of us watched as our speaking gigs, worth several thousand a pop, were canceled or indefinitely postponed. Others decided that we'd be back on the road sooner rather than later and actively said no to any virtual speaking. And there were those like myself, who bought proper stage lighting for our home offices, made our in-person talks fit for a tiny computer camera, and reached out to our in-person customers to say we were ready to serve them just as we'd promised. Then our pandemic spring became a pandemic fall, and then became spring again. More than 400,000 people had died, and nearly half of the United States had received one of the three different vaccines. It became safer to be social again, and my phone began ringing to book in-person events. I was already speaking a lot by that time, though. In the year we sheltered in place, I did my fourth TED Talk; launched a popular #BringYourWorth YouTube show scheduled every Monday, Wednesday, and Friday; and wrote, published, and keynoted my twenty-fifth book, *Build From Now: How to Know Your Power, See Your Abundance & Nourish the World*. I spoke more *and* my speaking price went up. The year 2020 was my busiest, most profitable speaking year. Imagine if I had actively decided to turn down virtual talks or, worse, sat paralyzed and made no decision at all? It's no judgment against those who wanted to wait it out, as none of us knew what was going to happen—which is my point. Taking a small risk in purchasing a few hundred dollars of professional equipment, spending an afternoon redesigning the office, and training a bit to speak sitting down rather than standing up totally transformed my career as well as the opportunities of many professional colleagues. I argue that the real risk is in not adapting at all. Despite the quarantine ease, most speaking events in 2021 were virtual instead of in-person. Folks who sat on the sidelines could be benched for not just one year, but two.

Peter Sims, author of *Little Bets: How Breakthrough Ideas Emerge from Small Discoveries*, writes: "Two fundamental advantages of the little bets approach are highlighted in the research of [University of Virginia] Professor Saras Sarasvathy: that it enables us to focus on what we can afford to lose rather than make assumptions about how much we can expect to gain, and that it facilitates the development of means as we progress with an idea." If we think in guarantees—"I'm not going to do this unless *I know* it will turn out to be a great decision"—then we will miss opportunities that take little effort and can potentially give us exponential returns. And if we focus too much on the *how*—"I'm not even sure about how to price this product, what the marketing will look like, and where it would be sold, so I'm not even going to research my idea"—then we miss the *why*. "At the beginning of any new idea, the possibilities can seem infinite, and that wide-open landscape of opportunity can become a prison of anxiety and self-doubt," Sims writes.

As Seth Godin puts it, starting will only get harder tomorrow. That particular spark, idea, or inspiration may not disappear completely, but it does have an expiration date—even though, in a cruel twist, you don't know when that expiration date will be. I'm not just talking about your big creative leaps. It could be the spark to break out on your own and start your own firm, the idea that you deserve better than the crappy job you've got, or the inspiration to do a simple side hustle to help make ends meet. And that expiration date could be a potential business partner moving on after you took too long to commit to the venture, a loved one suddenly needing resources that require you to stay put in that crappy job, or an unexpected market shift that makes your side hustle obsolete before you even start it. That's not to mention plain old inertia.

We may hang our hopes on the next business move, viewing it as our golden ticket out of unhappiness, but a Pollyanna approach actually pushes away our best opportunities. In short, it's too damn much pressure, and the higher your idealism toward the next step, the more inertia you have against moving at all. If you catch yourself using polarizing words like "I haven't found," "I absolutely need money to," or "I'm waiting for the right," then you may be viewing one simple business move as a panacea to your life's woes.

It won't be. Lower your expectations.

"The way through the challenge is to get still and ask yourself, 'What is the next right move?'" Oprah Winfrey said at a 2017 commencement speech. "Not think about 'Ooh, I got all of this to figure out.' What is the next right move? And then from that space, make the next right move and the next right move . . . then you won't be overwhelmed by it, because you know your life is bigger than that one moment."

Sociologist and *The Sweet Spot* author Dr. Christine Carter argues that we sometimes tie our happiness to improving our circumstances, but, in reality, the power is in finding meaning within our circumstances. If that's true, then our life goals should reflect what we need to *learn* rather than what we need to *change.*

"For high-achieving people, the big problem is confusing happiness with gratification. We've learned happiness is very fleeting. Getting meaning is more lasting, and meaning almost always leads to happiness. It's important to understand the difference," she told me. "It's important to know that meaning does not always lead to happiness, either—think about

Nelson Mandela. He probably gained a lot of meaning in his life, but probably was not happy when he was in prison."

You may never have been locked up, but being in a less-than-ideal job can certainly feel like it. The meaning behind the job still matters, though. Popular author Adam Grant told me about a job experience so traumatic that it led him into his most successful career decision: becoming an organizational psychologist. When I asked him what his mission had been before that, he said, "I don't know." He continued:

> I was studying psychology and was fascinated by all the ways we fail to understand our own minds: the bad decisions, the short-sighted moments, and all the ways we react when things go awry. Then I took an organizational psychology class and the light bulb suddenly went off. It was the things I was interested in, like motivating others and creating better teams, all to make work suck a little less. If we could redesign organizations and make them more meaningful, then we could improve all products and services. If anything progresses our way of life, it's done at work.

We don't always have control over our career experiences, but we do have complete agency over what lessons we decide to take from those experiences.

"High achievers often cut meaning out of their lives to achieve," Carter says. "They can do things to feel pleasure; but without meaning, they don't have the deep, lasting joy in the same way as when we have a sense of meaning."

It is why we aren't always willing to have short-term discomfort for long-term growth. Meaning takes time, sometimes pain, and, often, failure. Meaning requires reflection to fully integrate any lessons learned. And any worthwhile life goals are discovered when we are given what we don't want. Have you found deeper meaning in those moments when things went according to plan, or when you realized that you needed to do a course correction? Exactly.

The second step in setting your life goals is recognizing that your career is different from your job. Granted, you can have one job your entire life and have a fantastic career in that role or have multiple jobs and have a relatively lame career. They are really two different discussions.

The job is theirs. The career is yours.

To quote the late motivational speaker Jim Rohn, "If you work on your job, you'll make a living. If you work on yourself, you'll make a fortune."

It all ties back to Marie Forleo's philosophy: there is no such thing as wasted time. It's clear that her time as a cheerleader now helps her motivate coaching clients; as a bartender, sharpens her ability to quickly get to know other people; and as a hip-hop dance teacher, strengthens her stamina to do long keynotes and workshops. Her eponymous business has earned Forleo a literal financial fortune. We all have the opportunity to earn a deeper fortune, and that would come down to knowledge of self. If anything, your financial metrics will rise to mirror your self-knowledge, not the other way around. Money won't give you happiness, meaning, or insight. Self-knowledge can give you all three, though. You have to be willing to see the wisdom to be gained in your current role. Even if you don't like it.

Contrarily, complaining about your current status—or even being too satisfied with your role—can make you forget your power. If your job sucks and you spend your energy bitching about how awful it is, then you have decided to narrow your view and accept your fate. Indentured servitude aside, your job is not forever, but your career is. You're conflating the two. If your job is good enough and you save your energy from exploring anything beyond it, then you have also decided to narrow your view and accept your fate. To paraphrase CreativeLive co-founder Chase Jarvis, creativity is a muscle, and not flexing it will cause it to atrophy. Few things are as creative as envisioning a future where you'll be even closer to being your best self. It is the difference between Gay Hendricks's aforementioned comfortable zone of excellence, and the radical, unique zone of genius. You do not need to throw away everything, but even minor moves will help you stave off complacency.

"The only thing that is going to save you in this world is planning longer than other people," *The 48 Laws of Power* author Robert Greene told me, referencing Law 29: Plan All the Way to the End. "I mean, just knowing what's going to happen five years out, what you're meant to be doing with your life and what you're suited for. 'This crap job is not getting me there, so I'm leaving,' or 'I can't afford to leave this crap job, but I need to learn this on the side'—never treading water, but advancing somewhere."

Accepting where you are allows you to see the advantages of what you've got and, often, gain clarity on the proverbial Oprah next move. Years ago, a friend of mine told me I should become an entrepreneur. I laughed in their face. I was a journalist and an author. I *documented* Silicon Valley culture, I wasn't *in* it. Besides, I wasn't sure if the odd startup ideas I had in my head were actually worth anything—and, even if they were, whether I was the one to do them. They said, "I get it, but listen: you know the startup space well from all your reporting, you are self-funding your writing business, and you're used to being broke. Just like a bootstrapping founder!"

I started working on my first app, So Quotable, within the year.

Today, I am paid well for public speaking, receive steady royalty checks from my books, and have built a premium private-coaching practice. I have a wife, two kids, and a house. When my friend pulled me aside, literally none of this stuff existed. That conversation couldn't have happened now. And the friend was right: bootstrapping my two startups using guerrilla marketing techniques, serious networking, and frugal spending matched many of my skills groomed from my longtime freelance-writer career. More notably, though, is that the stretch from broke freelancer to low-resource founder was mild compared to the leap I'd have to make to do the same today. It is the expiration date on the opportunity. At the time, I absolutely wanted to make more money as a journalist; but, if I'd been financially flush, I'm positive I wouldn't have taken that career-defining risk. Sometimes the next step toward your life goal is in reach at the moment because your current job or business situation isn't ideal. As psychologist Christine Carter says, power is finding meaning exactly where you are.

Lastly, life goals have the most impact when you realize they will change. As they say in Silicon Valley, they are strong beliefs loosely held.

I share as much in *Bring Your Worth: Level Up Your Creative Power, Value & Service to the World*:

> If you haven't created a new baseline for your market value, what you're worth, and how you serve in five years, then you are making decisions based on who you were five years ago. Picture my kindergarten child holding the same values as an infant, or your 30-year-old self making the same choices as your 25-year-old self. It is ridiculous, at best. And yet, we create these magnificent, epic careers doing our thing, and do not take the time to actually see why we're doing this thing, how we are being valued for doing this thing, and what we're contributing by continually doing this thing.

For Forleo, her business shifted from personal—about helping others to make sure they were OK—to visionary—giving to others because she knows what it's like not to be OK.

"I had pain early on," Forleo says, "seeing my parents divorce, the perception of losing their love, and seeing my family falling apart. I told myself, 'I need to be successful one day, so I can take care of people[,] and financial resources wouldn't be the reason that love would be taken away.'"

"My definition of security has expanded over the years, though," she adds. "As I've matured, we've grown our platform, the ways we use our platform, and how we provide tools and strategies to get out of pain. How can I share that?"

It comes full circle, as facing and accepting the discomfort of her earliest years gave her meaning, not only to help heal herself but also to heal others. Perhaps that self-healing wouldn't have occurred without creating the tools and strategies she did to uplift others. She could have easily kept the first life goal—"I need to be successful one day, so I can take care of people and so financial resources wouldn't be the reason that love would be taken away." The main objective would be to get, save, or perhaps even hoard money. But there's no way she would have explored the odd jobs, found deeper meaning in her far-from-payday experiences, and made the investment to launch her coaching platform. To make her world today, she had to evolve.

Holding stubbornly to your life goals won't guarantee success or even progress. Being vigilant in how and why you want to serve, though, is a north star you want to keep. It is putting message over medium. If you are staying true to whom you want to serve, then your life goals will naturally grow to encompass all the brilliant ways you can bring your worth. By not holding too tightly, you are making room for genius opportunities beyond your current scope of vision.

→

II.

UNCOVER POWER IN YOUR OWN TOOLBOX

A lifetime of brainwashing has taught us that work is about measurable results, that failure is fatal, and that we should be sure that the recipe is proven before we begin. And so we bury our dreams. We allow others to live in our head, reminding us that we are impostors with no hope of making an original contribution.

—Seth Godin

Many of us learned when we were young, perhaps around the age of my elementary-school kids, that a tree's roots grow as deep as the tree is tall. I remember seeing photos of redwoods and similar trees, imagining their roots extending to the center of the Earth like some medieval painting. In coaching circles, this is a common analogy for showing that the deeper we go, the higher we climb.

Unfortunately, it's a myth.

Arborists—that is, tree experts—say the tree roots actually don't have to go that far down to get the best nutrients which, counterintuitively, are in the soil just a few feet below the surface.

What a tree really needs, though, isn't depth: it needs *range*.

"A tree's root system is unlikely ever to be more than a couple of feet down," wrote one expert. "But its spread can easily be as wide as the tree's crown."

We can look at our proverbial toolbox and see a bunch of junk. Now, there is an experience that was once useful, but I consider it a failure. Another thing I learned that—what is that?—I don't even know what to do with it, so it must be useless. A bag of knowledge that doesn't seem to fit any of the other parts. We may only find one tool we value, and we feel utterly disappointed that it doesn't fix all situations. Meanwhile, we have many other equally rich tools that we aren't valuing.

This is a side effect of a past culture we're still reckoning. If you invest four years of your life and a quarter million dollars in this piece of paper, then you don't have to worry about your career. Give your weekends, jeopardize your health, and practically sell your soul to this unethical company, and you'll make so much money that you'll be able to make up for any damage done by "giving back later." You can go on autopilot. Just sacrifice everything else for this one tool.

For young Generation Xers like myself, we saw our grandparents (just like their parents, and perhaps their parents before them) make this Faustian bargain for security and, often, for the love of their family. Then we saw our parents make the same pact, but the economy shifted from white-and-blue collar to knowledge worker right under their feet. The devil reneged when our parents sacrificed enough to lose some of their most productive years, but too soon before the gold watch and guaranteed pension. We saw this, rebelling against working at all—the term "slacker" is the word I remember hearing most during my late teenage years—but still we weren't sure how to change our fate. And the next generations are now assuming that everything is unstable.

But all of us are still struggling to reframe our power. Whether it is going to an Ivy League school or going viral on TikTok, we are still looking to be picked—by the good jobs, by the tastemakers—rather than picking ourselves. We lean on one tool, one exit, one socially accepted road to success, because it feels safer than exploring all our tools and potentially stumbling, feeling out of control or, perhaps worst of all, being ostracized. "Our commitment to the process is the only alternative to the lottery mindset of hoping for the good luck of getting picked by the universe," Seth Godin says. In *The Practice: Shipping Creative Work*, he argues that true power lies not in knowing you are going to win, but in the practice of showing up as your best self. Not unlike fishing. "At some point," Godin says, "the professional has to bring home the fish. That's the fuel that permits the professional to show up every day. But the catch is the side effect of the practice itself. Get the practice right, and your commitment will open the door for the market to engage with your work. When Elizabeth King said, 'Process saves us from the poverty of our intentions,' she was talking about the fish. You might seek a shortcut, a hustle, a way to somehow cajole that fish onto the hook. But if it distracts you from the process, your art will suffer. Better to set aside judging yourself until after you've committed to the practice and done the work."

We need to understand that the work cannot get deep until you actually see what's in your toolbox. First, you have to recognize your strengths. They often don't come from our experiences, but they are *revealed* in our experiences, which is why you can go through the same journey as another and have two very different outcomes. What matters is the meaning we assign to our moments. Second, we should tie past decisions to future growth. We have very few singular decisions that are life-changing. Everything we decide, though, changes the odds of something happening or not happening later. If we aren't feeling empowered, then we must go backward to go forward. Lastly, we must make room for growth. Coming into your power is a lot harder when you barely have enough time to respond to—let alone strategize—your life. You have to commit to making space now to empower yourself tomorrow.

And the wider the breadth of knowledge you have in your own power, the easier it will be to wear your crown.

CHAPTER 4.

RECOGNIZE AND MINE YOUR BIGGEST ESTABLISHED STRENGTHS

I've had a lifelong interest in personality-assessment tools. Well, it may be closer to an obsession. As a teenager, I discovered the Myers-Briggs assessment and took it almost every year to see how my filter changed. Later, I became fascinated with the Gallup StrengthsFinder, Sally Hogshead's Fascinate model, Gretchen Rubin's Four Tendencies, and other modern-day approaches. I even studied perhaps the most mystical assessment: astrology. (My astrology work actually helped make ends meet early in my freelance career, with dispensing Mercury Retrograde and Sun in Scorpio wisdom sometimes making more money than my traditional journalism.)

I now understand the desire in my quest: objectivity. How do you know your power? When do you recognize that you are being your highest self? Where should you be heading in your career, if not your life? To paraphrase Dad 2.0 founders Doug French and Jeff Bogle, you can't read the label when you're inside the jar.

As a coach, I've found that the biggest challenge to understanding our strengths is separating the environment from the individual. I get now that it isn't possible. Simon Sinek, Adam Grant, and other leadership experts cite study after study that confirm it. Star sport players reach legendary numbers and break longtime records, so other teams make a ridiculously expensive trade to get them on their squad.

Powerhouse doctors do shining work at their clinics, and other hospitals court them to head their medical programs. Lead singers do sell-out tours as the face of a group, and soon record labels are offering them beaucoup bucks for a solo deal. The commonality, of course, is that their success is at a minimum symbiotic with the group—and may actually be *because* of the group. Last year's breakout quarterback completed those amazing passes for a record number of touchdowns and brilliant completions because he had someone exceptional catching the ball, defending his run, or strategizing his play. The smart surgeon did strong work because her more-than-capable nurses and surgical team gave her so much support, she didn't have to worry about anything but the patient. The music front man's golden voice is perfectly captured within the flavor of the group, and missing one or more elements will resonate differently with the loyal fans. It doesn't diminish the talent of any of these leaders. What it does do is show that context matters, and in understanding your personal power you must factor in where you are putting that power, how that power is supported, and who is giving you a framework for that power.

"It's popular, especially in Western cultures, for people to think of themselves as 'self-made,' but their full selves are actually built by and shaped by interactions with others. Compared to any other being, we humans spend the longest amount of time in childhood during which we learn from others and how to become like others, benefiting from the inventions and creativity of previous generations," Nilofer Merchant says in *The Power of Onlyness: Make Your Wild Ideas Mighty Enough to Dent the World.*

It's a tale as old as time, from Oedipus to Luke Skywalker: we all suffer from what's called a responsibility bias, overvaluing our own contributions to our success and undervaluing how others have added to our worth. You know how hard you worked to get where you've gotten. That's clear as day.

You know what you sacrificed! But what did your mom do? Or your supervisor who gave you the benefit of the doubt? Or those hidden or forgotten allies who, as we'll get into later in the book, are speaking your name in rooms that you don't usually have access to?

"We can have intense, often overwhelming clarity on the work ahead, but it can take us a while to recognize the work done by our predecessors before we got here," I share in *Build From Now: How to Know Your Power, See Your Abundance & Nourish the World*. "Like a child discovering something new and believing she is the first to find it, we don't always see that people have walked the path we're on. They may have made our path clearer. Without them, the path may not even exist."

I often tell my clients that it isn't the scars from what happened to you, but the lessons that you decide to learn from it that create who you will become. That part is our responsibility. That part is in our control. If you suffer a broken heart, you can choose to protect what you've got left, remember that the high risk is part of the high reward, or accept your role in the relationship and heal to be open for the next time you fall in love. It's why I applaud whenever my boys get up from a fall.

Everyone falls, but how did you land?

In *The Power of Onlyness*, Merchant shares a fascinating take from Yale professor Nicholas Christakis. "He points out that both pencil lead (graphite) and diamonds are composed of carbon. But their constituent atoms have been exposed to different degrees of heat or pressure, which affects how they connect to their neighboring atoms." What we take out of an experience is ours and ours alone. Merchant recommends separating the event from the meaning. Yes, this thing happened, but it is possible to view something neither as a victim nor as a perpetrator. You can look at it as an observer. In other words, the meaning you extract from an experience is always and completely under your control. And if meaning molds your strengths, then how you grow is always and completely under your control too.

I found my own framework for this after coaching hundreds of side hustlers, solopreneurs, and other non-traditional entrepreneurs. As I explain in *Build From Now: How to Know Your Power, See Your Abundance & Nourish the World*, I noticed that each and every one of us has the same four resources: Focus, Agility, Time, and Energy. I call them the F.A.T.E.s for short. We all have the ability to focus, be agile in new situations, spend time on our craft, and burn energy going toward an important goal. One particular resource may be higher for you, while another may be lacking. But we often don't see our biggest resources available, because we're so focused on what we lack and so blind to our strongest assets. We take for granted the powers we've always had, as we'll talk about more later. For now, the most important thing to understand is that our F.A.T.E.s are molded by our environment and perhaps even our personality, but we often fail to recognize them because they are ever-changing.

You can find the *Build From Now* quiz right now in the back of the book. Feel free to do the quick assessment, then flip back to here.

In *Build From Now*, I explain the constant feedback between self, environment, and habit:

> Our lives are like the grooves of a vinyl record. They begin smooth and impressionable, like a black acetate. Over time, the feedback of our environment and the call of our needs create habits. The needle falls into the groove, making the patterns more ingrained. Even when we direct the needle elsewhere, it naturally falls from the peak into the comfortable valley. What we often forget is that our best grooves are ever-changing. These grooves are animated, ebbing and flowing based on where we are and who we are. They are far from static. They are alive . . . you can look at these resources like levers: they aren't absolutes, and they operate independently of

each other. You may have a brief period where all four are at their peak. More often, though, one trait will be particularly high and at least one particularly low.

It addressed one of the common misapprehensions of today: that we need to be fixed. You should do this life hack to be your best every day. You better do the same as this random entrepreneur, or you're wasting your life away. This is the way, and the only way, to be your best self right now. Self-improvement culture is one passionate "guru" away from religious dogma. And like any dogma, the secret is that your inner wisdom is just as pure as, and way more specific than, any strict teachings a self-appointed leader could give you. Empowerment isn't finding the parts of you that are broken and turning them in for repair. Empowerment is realizing that those cracks, overlaps, and scars are your keys to power. The only thing we can gain from believing we are broken is shame.

"You can't shame your way to success," I said on the #BringYourWorth show episode "How to Fail Well (Brené Brown quote)." "Shame isn't going to get us there. It's not going to make us more productive. It's not going to make our stuff more fruitful. And it's definitely not going to give us success. The main thing shame does is actually quieting our inner voice because we're so worried about what other people are going to say."

"You will need the confidence to say no to those who attempt to define something that is inherently yours," Merchant writes in *The Power of Onlyness*. You are the one who must assign meaning to your path. Otherwise, a meaning will be assigned to you. It's better to own those abundances and valleys, and those scars and those halos, than to give away your power of meaning to someone or something else.

➡

CHAPTER 5.

TRANSLATE PAST POWER INTO FUTURE SUCCESS

I t is empowering not only to objectively give your experiences meaning but also to determine what informed those decisions you made within those experiences. In my practice, I've found that our biggest resources often come from survival. I moved a lot growing up and had to quickly figure out how I fit in within new environments, what cultural norms dominated the area, and how to socially survive in each situation. It's no doubt affected how I ask incisive questions (journalism), stay curious about how other people operate (coaching), and manage to make connections most everywhere I go (cultural writing and traveling). The longer we go into our careers, the more we can believe that thriving in a certain job brought about these traits—for example, getting two degrees in journalism made me more inquisitive. But my coaching experience has shown me that this simply isn't true. If anything, it is the reverse: our chosen professions reflect our survival traits and, at best, reinforce what's already underneath the surface. When we don't like a particular job or opportunity that we chose, it can reflect those particular learned traits that we haven't accepted or that have outgrown their usefulness. It can be like an intimate relationship where we unconsciously project our fears, needs, and traumas that we won't accept onto someone or something that fits—what psychologist Carl Jung would call "the other"—until we begin to integrate those shadow pieces into ourselves. And suddenly, the attraction is gone. The relationship doesn't fulfill us anymore. Perhaps we can look at our being dissatisfied with a current job not as a failure but as a healing of the self that needed validation in a very specific way.

Psychologists call these survival traits "coping mechanisms." We often call them our personality! When we do this categorization, though, we miss the opportunity to actually alchemize our past self into something healthier than before. "That's just the way I am" is the language of disempowering your present and future self. And because we are in a constant relationship with our environment, both old and current, we can extend this disempowerment to the culture, norms, and trauma we've experienced within them.

"Claiming your spot is not just about recounting one's history and experience, but about defining what that history and experience have come to mean to you," Nilofer Merchant writes in *The Power of Onlyness*. "What did you say no (or yes) to, whom did you decide to support or reject, and what did you decide to persist with, despite pressures to stop? These decisions define and form your puzzle piece into its own distinct shape."

I would argue that you should take pride in your own distinct shape. But, as Merchant implies, that requires you to own what created your distinct shape in the first place. We can leave a trail of strong lessons, tough breaks, and big opportunities that helped make us who we are today—and leave the gems behind because we don't want to acknowledge *any* of the time we spent on the journey. It's easier to just not talk about it. Besides, it is done. But as *The Hero with a Thousand Faces* author Joseph Campbell said, "The cave you fear to enter holds the treasure you seek."

"As a coach, I instinctively get chills when I hear someone talk about 'starting over,' getting a 'clean slate,' or 'erasing the past.' That isn't even possible," I admit in *Build From Now*. "As the classic saying goes, 'No matter where you go, there you are." Eventually, you're going to have to do that work." In the *Build From Now* predecessor *Bring Your Worth: Level Up Your Creative Power, Value & Service to the World*, I explain why we often disregard how much things have shaped us—we're afraid to give them power:

> Picture scaffolding, but instead of from the inside out, picture it going from the outside in. It is our bones, our literal integrity, which difficult times test and fortify. Without challenging ourselves, we do not know if the values we created are really what we believe. The universe, which really means you, since you are one with the world, does not create struggle to punish you, but to reconfirm what you actually believe. The confidence to know what you believe isn't complete until you are given ample opportunity to disregard it.

In the previous chapter, Recognize and Mine Your Biggest Established Strengths, we realized that you need context from your environment to better understand your assets. Similarly, you also don't really know what you stand for until you notice what you aren't. Deciding to do this but not that isn't just some random choice you made out of naïveté, nor is your current position in life and career some divine accident. Pressurized situations, forks in the road, and other often-binary moments bring out our values. Not the best or the worst out of us—they just bring out what we deem most important: security or adventure; freedom or structure; experiment or status quo. (And even these examples have shades of gray, like how you may be terrified to say "Hi" to someone first, but may jump out of an airplane [with a parachute, we hope] without giving it a second thought. We'll talk more about how we evaluate risk and security in chapter 12, Lean Into Steady Growth [Without Losing Your Shirt].) Realizing that we have been deciding based on our values all along not only helps us refine them but also helps us notice that we have more control than we think. Circumstances don't just make us: they also help reveal us.

"Systems are machines that determine probability," business author Dan Heath says in *Upstream: The Quest to Solve Problems Before They Happen.* Systems can be the way we structure our household, run our business, or otherwise operate within a culture, as we talk about in part VI, Build Systems to Bulletproof Your Career. However, the systems we create, allow, or perpetuate are reflective of our own filter often created in the past. Otherwise, we wouldn't accept the system at all. And if you don't know what filters you have, then you don't know what—or why!— you are creating, allowing, or perpetuating a particular system. This ties into your outcomes because, as Heath writes, your systems, and therefore your filter on life, determine what you'll get. For instance, if you are afraid that you won't get your share, then you are more likely to take more than your share in collaborations—pushing away potentially fair collaborators and turning yourself into the very type of person you fear. (Adam Grant's *Give and Take: Why Helping Others Drives Our Success* outlines this theory beautifully, as we'll talk about later in the book.) But without knowing our filter and recognizing how the past has molded us, we may not recognize that we have this fear. All we know is that we keep getting shitty collaborators.

If we want to improve the outcome, then we first need to go backward and recognize, respect, and honor our own lessons from the past. It is only then that we'll begin to trust our vision to others, because we would have begun to trust ourselves. How can you trust those inner voices, those instincts, if some of those voices scare you? Those gut feelings aren't just informed by your trauma, but they also can direct you to your healing. Refusing to look at your past shuts down all the voices, preventing you from fully investing in yourself and, as a consequence, in others.

Integrating your past is a slow process worth pursuing. It will give you more peace of mind. It also unlocks the energy you need to reach your best career goals and aspirations.

"There are people and organizations in our lives that we trust. How did that happen? We develop trust over time. Our interactions lead to expectations, and those expectations, repeated and supported, turn into trust," Seth Godin says in *The Practice: Shipping Creative Work*. "These organizations and people earn trust by coming through in the difficult moments. They're not perfect; in fact, the way they deal with imperfection is precisely why we trust them. We can do the same thing to (and with) ourselves. As we engage in the practice, we begin to trust the practice. Not that it will produce the desired outcome each time, but simply that it's our best available option. Trust earns you patience, because once you trust yourself, you can stick with a practice that most people can't handle."

➡

CHAPTER 6.

MAKE ROOM FOR YOUR WISDOM

We may know our strengths and can even see where our filters have benefited and hobbled us. To quote leadership coach Marshall Goldsmith, "What got you here won't get you there." The next level of understanding is to actually make the room to change. We can be so consumed with efficiency that we don't give ourselves space to think, experiment, and explore new methods. We can be so reactionary that we don't actually initiate anything.

"The problem is obvious—if you spend all day hitting the ball back, you'll never end up serving," Seth Godin says in *The Practice: Shipping Creative Work*. If you do not know your intentions beyond your environment, then it's ridiculously easy for the values of that environment to dominate your actions. We all have a sprinkle of innovation, a dash of risk, or a bucket of rebellion to bring into the cultures we inhabit. "But you weren't meant to blend in. You were meant to rebuild," I write in *Build From Now: How to Know Your Power, See Your Abundance & Nourish the World*. "Otherwise, why are you here?"

One of the biggest ways to rediscover our initiative is to reclaim our time. Time is one of the four resources in my *Build From Now* framework—Focus, Agility, Time, and Energy. In the context of that book, though, time is a resource whose abundance or lack thereof we recognize based on our current life circumstances, not something we are seeing usurped by outside forces. It's like checking the thermometer versus being in a hothouse—one tells you what's going on, while the other is actually making it happen.

When I talked to concentration management expert Cal Newport, he told me things have gotten worse, since we are now used to being hyperconnected to our organizations, our communities, and even to ourselves. In *A World Without Email: Reimagining Work in an Age of Communication Overload*, he says the more we leaned into technology to empower our independence, from having a personal computer to modern-day working from home, the more technology artificially inflated our need to be hyperconnected to everything else. Newport calls this the "hyperactive hive mind": why we check our phone every thirty seconds, obsessively peek in our inbox, and feel ghost notification buzzes in our pocket with or without our phone.

This cultural shift is a one-way street. "Once you decide the main way we organize all work is informal, unscheduled back-and-forth messaging, you're always going to have that messaging going on," he told me. It's the equivalent of regularly answering a colleague's, supervisor's, or client's email on a Sunday afternoon—you've now created, allowed, or perpetuated a particular system, as we discussed in the last chapter.

In *A World Without Email*, Newport shares my new favorite term: digital sunsets. In short, this is when you cut off communication to your business: 5:00 p.m. every weekday, during every weekend, and so on. Do you even turn off your business? I didn't during the year and a half sheltering in place, and I've been feeling the strain during pandemic homeschooling, book launching, and lots of virtual coaching for my clients. Simply put, I've been always available. Newport suggests installing an off switch for when and how you're available. It absolutely requires the input of your leadership above and below you. Culturally, you'll have to get your customers used to the new availability, especially as competitors may be offering something more robust. The benefit, though, is better long-term value for those you serve. It allows a deeper focus for how you and your business show up, even during the pandemic chaos. Take the time to think about how you show up from top to bottom.

Another way to make room for growth is to—ironically—better accept who you are and honor how you show up. Entrepreneur and consultant Julian Mitchell has a wonderful saying: "Get paid to be yourself." Read over the motto carefully. It isn't "get rich or die trying"—no offense to rapper 50 Cent—which says you're willing to do anything for the dough. Being obsessed with one outcome makes it easy to compromise your integrity. The real danger is that it doesn't happen in one fateful decision, but as a slow compromise of your values as opportunities require you to cross your boundaries inch by inch. And we often don't notice. *Upstream* author Dan Heath calls this "unintentional blindness: our careful attention to one task leads us to miss important information that's related to that task." Mitchell's saying also isn't "just be yourself," as that doesn't have any service component. It took me a long time to realize this in my own career, if not in my own life. On one extreme, you may be totally shameless in how you show up, even as you disserve or even violate others. I've seen teachers, coaches, and other leaders rip people in their community apart under the guise of just "being themselves" and "telling it like it is." As I say in the preceding chapter, Translate Past Power into Future Success, "That's just the way I am" is the language of disempowering your present and future self—and, because we are in a constant relationship with our environment both old and current, we can extend this disempowerment to the culture, norms, and trauma we've experienced within them. People who say this are wounded. On the other extreme, being yourself may mean giving your all without any expectations in return. My book *Bring Your Worth: Level Up Your Creative Power, Value & Service to the World* came from my struggle with this: If you are doing your life's work, then isn't that enough payment? No, it isn't. Bills and other practical considerations aside, not getting your worth in money, services, or other appropriate transactions creates a cultural norm for the people you serve. Your work is expendable. It is available on tap whenever I need it, though I never have to pay the tab. It is like accidentally spilling a drink at an open bar—it sucks for exactly one second, and then you remember you can just belly up and get another one. Like the get-rich-or-die-trying approach, the be-yourself-and-just-serve mentality will have your boundaries eroding interaction after interaction until, in some cases, you demand to be respected and honored properly—financially or otherwise.

It's worth noting that I've had many conversations with clients who believe making their new product, service, or idea cheaper than it should be will build goodwill and long-term sales with their potential customers. It doesn't. First, by underpricing your product, you're increasing the chances of *your* going under—and then you'll be of no use to anyone. Worse, you'll have no margin for special sales and pricing changes, or, ironically, won't be able to afford to serve the people at a discount who actually need it. Second, if you underprice what you've got, you raise an unspoken suspicion in your potential customers. So you're a four-time TED speaker, best-selling author, and exited (sold) your last startup, but you're charging $20 for an hour-long coaching session? Less than a family-of-four meal at a fast-food joint? Either you're lying about your history or you're going to try to immediately upsell me for the *real* coaching. Hard pass. The way through is to take the Seth Godin approach: I charge a premium, but what I'm offering will give you ten times (or, as entrepreneurs call it, 10x) the value. Dropping the price signals that the price is your only leverage. You're not McDonald's.

"Get paid to be yourself" means taking the best you have to offer to those who honor your service the most. I've gotten a nice check after an awful experience, and I've done some of my best work in non-financially sustainable arrangements. Neither is ideal. And, as *Pivot* author Jenny Blake says, you can have the joy *and* the money.

The last recommendation to make room in your life is simple: be still. Doing meditation or another mindfulness practice is great. What I mean, though, is not feeling like every action, event, or moment requires your reaction. "The greatest victory is that which requires no battle," Sun Tzu says in *The Art of War*. The goal should be to *conserve* your energy, not to flex it on your so-called foes, and this gives you the power to turn up the volume when required. As we'll talk about in chapter 13, Measure Your Results and Adjust as Necessary, everything follows a cycle just like nature. And if you react to every slight, chest puff, or throat-clearing gesture, then you'll be worn down.

Stoic historians Ryan Holiday and Stephen Hanselman capture this well: I do not need to have an opinion on everything. The authors' *The Daily Stoic: 366 Meditations on Wisdom, Perseverance, and the Art of Living* is really an ode to this philosophy. Pinging back to Newport's "hyperactive hive mind" argument, do we need to be outraged at the latest thing trending on social media? How successful is arguing with someone who is saying things just to knock you off your game? When was the last time a shouting match actually got either of you—or all of you!—closer to your goal? I left Facebook and other platforms because the ratio of shouting versus communicating skyrocketed, but even taking the Cal Newport approach (who himself doesn't do social media at all) only protects you so much from the distractions. And I've found that the more circles you traverse, the more you need to be able to manage your own ego.

All three challenges are tied to one trait natural to just being human: storytelling. We tell ourselves a narrative about how much time we've got, we tell ourselves a story about whether we will be accepted for who we are, and we tell ourselves a tale about how we can't let even one slight slide. We can be so eager to create a narrative, we often begin telling ourselves a story before we even have all the important details. "We're wired for story and in the absence of data we will rely on confabulations and conspiracies," emotional intelligence pioneer Brené Brown says in *Rising Strong: How the Ability to Reset Transforms the Way We Live, Love, Parent, and Lead*. "More information means less fear-based story-making."

We can reclaim our power with three words: "I don't know." We may not know how to maximize our time yet, whether our shared community will accept us as our full selves, or whether what rubs us the wrong way is because of our ego or because of our insight. The problem is that, as leaders of ourselves and potentially others, we feel that we should know—otherwise, why are we leaders?

Leadership isn't about knowing everything when you need it, but knowing when you don't have enough information to go forward. You lead because of your vision, your insight, and your bravery, not because of your ESP. You are in good shape, as long as you make and keep enough room to grow into your next role.

→

III.

DISCOVER ECONOMIC OPPORTUNITIES IN THE NEW WORLD ORDER

"The future is here. It's just not evenly distributed."

—William Gibson

ne of my favorite psychology jokes is: "There are five frogs on a log. One of them decided to jump off. How many are on the log now? Five." Wanting and even saying you want to do something isn't the same as actually doing it. The classic joke is funny—at least, to me—because it reminds us how the most meticulous plan has as much value as a slipshod idea until, and unless, something is actually executed.

As popular science fiction author William Gibson says above, we don't all have the same access. He may have meant quite literally: in 2003, I remember visiting Tokyo's Akihabara district, the digital billboard, high-tech–strewn place that inspired the look of fellow sci-fi writer Philip K. Dick's movie *Blade Runner*. I was saucer-eyed, awestruck, and overstimulated the entire time. What struck me the most, though, was how everyone was glued to their cell phone: while walking, while talking, while eating. If I hadn't moved fast enough, some folks would have run me right off the crowded sidewalks. I came back home to Chicago and felt almost relieved that no one seemed as obsessed with being on their phone—if they had one at all. Cellular phones (people still called them by their full name back then) were expensive, it cost you money when other people called *you*, and you almost unconsciously would stand as still as possible when you did get a call for fear of it being dropped. I blinked, Apple launched the iPhone, and suddenly every major American city I visited felt just like the Akihabara district had a half decade earlier. I *did* step into the future. I just didn't realize it—or, at best, didn't think it would be here so soon.

Gibson's take applies not just to technology but to our vision too. The business opportunities you see depend on where you sit, how you filter, and what you have access to. For instance, I have close family in the rougher parts of South Jersey, lived by and in some tough neighborhoods across the country, and have friends who tightrope on the poverty line. But I also went to the number one journalism school in the country, have spoken to the ultra-wealthy at the TED Conference, and have friends who are millionaire entrepreneurs. I know genius lies in the ghetto and in the gold rooms. When I moved to Silicon Valley, though, many folks I met associated an Ivy League degree with capability, a straight white male identity with credibility, and a set of zip codes with the value of one's ideas. I recognized that brilliant, non-traditional entrepreneurs lived everywhere outside of Silicon Valley, too—because I knew them! And while the Bay Area didn't see that vision, I began writing books, doing talks, and building a coaching practice around them. And, recognizing how mobile my own influence had been while I moved from coast to coast and all in between, I knew the entrepreneur ecosystems would grow in other areas, too. Like Tokyo, Silicon Valley was the future—but they didn't realize that the rest of the country would be the future too.

Then the pandemic hit. Everyone needed to work virtually, which meant it didn't matter where you lived. The very expensive Bay Area had one of the biggest population drops in the country. And everyone suddenly seemed equal.

"VCs who once spurned [Midwest city Indianapolis, Indiana] because they couldn't get there and back from the West Coast in a day are now airlifting cash into the city—not to mention Atlanta, Miami, Denver, and other towns that were never on their short-list before," *Inc.* magazine wrote at the time. As one funder told Editor-at-Large Bill Saporito, "When you have a total and absolute moratorium on physical travel, yet those dollars are being deployed, almost overnight things change."

You're now reading my seventh book for these same non-traditional entrepreneurs, starting with the best seller *The Bite-Sized Entrepreneur* in 2016. I left Silicon Valley a decade ago. What would have happened if I'd waited for everyone else to see the future I saw?

We all have a unique cultural vantage point based on our experiences, our networks, and our passions. In each of us, it creates a one-of-a-kind kaleidoscopic view. There are certain ways to serve a specific community, make money with an idea, and fill a particular gap that only you can see. In marketing, they call it the "white space." Who isn't being served, and how can you show up for them?

Like the frogs on a log, though, recognizing a white space isn't enough to make a brilliant business move, let alone make an impact. As we'll talk about, there are three steps that can help you pursue your best opportunities right now: assessing the business landscape; pivoting based on worldly circumstances; and strategizing your first move and ultimate goals. First, you have to see how people are already being served, as well as being honest about the best ways for you to show up in today's environment. In a simple example, if my co-founders and I had launched our popular hugging app Cuddlr in September 2020 instead of September 2014, then our product would have had a *slightly* different response. Second, it is wise to adjust your execution based on what makes sense now, not based on the hypothetical plan in your head. Lastly, strategizing your first and last moves allows you to bookend all the planning from A to Z.

The ultimate goal is for you to trust your vision. Once you recognize and honor your unique viewpoint, then you understand it is your responsibility to execute it and share it with the world. Otherwise, you're just another frog on the log—and that singular vision eventually dies with you.

CHAPTER 7.

ASSESS THE BUSINESS LANDSCAPE

Y ou could be in a bad job, perhaps made a wrong turn somewhere in your career, or even be stewing in what people nowadays call a "toxic" environment. But we often don't know what's going on outside the fishbowl in which we swim. In other words, no matter how awful your position, you may be capped at only having an inkling of how poor the situation suits you because you—and all of us—can only be sure that *out there* is actually better.

As we talked about in chapter 2, Make Your Own Metrics for Success, understanding your personal strengths, assets, and power goes a long way toward seeing whether others value you. Once you know your own worth, then you'll immediately notice when the environment doesn't recognize it. But even admitting that requires you to actually recognize your role in the affair. After all, you are the one who asked for the job interview, had a conversation with the organization, and said, "Yes, this is the next best step in my career!"—or, at minimum, "Yes, this will do." Once we recognize our own worth, we then may have to face our self-betrayal—not just potentially that of the organization. We have to learn to trust ourselves again. And until that reckoning happens, we can never make peace with our future decisions either.

Our reluctance to admit that we miscalculated when we said yes can feel like an ego Catch-22. We say our job sucks, but we're the ones who signed up for the tour of duty in the first place, which means that our judgment sucks. We say it's not that bad, but that means we end up sticking around in stagnant—if not retrograde—situations to prove that we are solid in our decision-making.

We could end up not seeing better business opportunities because we are too busy licking our wounds or defending our past decisions.

"Escalation of commitment happens in every workplace," workplace psychologist Adam Grant says on his TED podcast, WorkLife. "Think about the times when you over-invested in a failing project, stuck around in a miserable job, struggled to walk away from an abusive boss or a toxic culture—or even, away from work, poured your heart and soul into a romantic relationship that clearly wasn't working. So why don't we know better? Why do we fall into the same trap again and again, pouring more and more of ourselves into a bad decision, even when all the evidence points us the other way? The most common answer people give—sunk costs. We've already invested our time or money, and we want to do everything in our power to get a return on that investment . . . but decades of research show that the most powerful forces aren't economic—they're emotional."

"It's not just a cold calculation of the loss of money or time," Grant summarizes. "It's the hot pain of threats to our sense of self."

These "threats to our sense of self" can have us missing key business opportunities to shine brighter—or could just stagnate us right out of our profession. We assume that if we stand still, we'll be able to keep our status, security, and job. We assume the only thing we need to do is withstand the pain of our uncomfortable environment and we'll be fine until we're ready to change (which is, often, "tomorrow"). Our careers aren't static, though. They are more like the stock market or, more accurately, the American dollar: there is a natural inflation that happens no matter what. That $10,000 you have stuffed underneath the mattress will be worth about $5,000 a decade from now. The only way to combat inflation is to invest and get returns: a savings account, a stock, a bond, and so on. As investors say, you don't invest to get rich quickly, but to not go poor slowly. Your deciding not to change is a decision that just gets harder as time goes on.

"One of the benefits of our past experiences in the tech world is needing to learn to react quickly to new market realities. You are forced to constantly deal with ambiguity. So, in a way, we were trained and prepared to adapt to a completely new trend in the spirit world," Austin Craft Spirits co-founder Stephan Godevais told me. He, along with fellow tech veterans Gary Kotshott and Tom Buchsbaum, decided to start a spirits company to ease into "retirement." They strategized the launch for their signature Austin 101 light whiskey—for spring 2020. Bars closed. Partyers stayed home. Even SXSW, the ridiculously influential conference in their back yard, called it quits for the year.

The sunk costs here weren't the resources they invested—Godevais told me they kept costs extremely low anyway and, according to an interview in Jeanette Hurt's *Forbes* magazine spirits column, "Instead of investing in equipment, they rent equipment from other craft distillers who are not running at capacity, but they do have their own aging facility so they can properly age their whiskey and then bottle it as soon as it reaches the flavor profile they desire."

Rather, their sunk costs were letting go of the commitment to a specific experience. They were not going to have in-person tastings. They would not be sponsoring large concerts and events. They had to let go of "perfect," to adapt to the business environment. Unfortunately, he says, many traditionalists in their industry could not:

The pandemic had dramatically different effects on the business of mainstream and craft distillers. While mainstream brands saw a huge uptick in their sales, craft distillers suffered severe business losses.

The main reason is that craft distillers rely primarily on product tastings and shelf appeal to promote their product and convert tastings into sales. The pandemic halted in-store tastings instantly and consumers didn't spend time anymore walking the aisles to explore new craft whiskeys. Although retail tastings will eventually resume, the marketing landscape for the craft distillers who survive will look very different and online presence will be a more important component of distillers' strategies than it has been so far.

In grafting our past decisions onto today's world, we miss the opportunity to grow into a better version of our business, our career, and ourselves. As I share in the previous Set Your Life Goals chapter (chapter 4), I had a parallel experience in the public-speaking realm: "Some of us watched as our speaking gigs, worth several thousand a pop, were canceled or indefinitely postponed. Others decided that we'd be back on the road sooner rather than later and actively said no to any virtual speaking. And there were those like myself, who bought proper stage lighting for our home offices, made our in-person talks fit for a tiny computer camera, and reached out to our in-person customers to say we were ready to serve them just as we promised."

Austin Craft Spirits prospered during the pandemic because the founders allowed themselves to grow according to now, not yesterday, and definitely not to the idealized plan they had once had in their minds.

"Thank you, Zoom, Instagram, Google, and Facebook. Without you guys, we wouldn't be around right now," Godevais told me. "We use social media platforms to keep our fan base and customers informed, do giveaways, promote inviting stories on Instagram such as the Austin 101 summer cocktail series and post virtual tastings videos. . . . We're [looking at holding] five to ten virtual tastings a week."

Keep in mind that virtual tastings didn't really exist before March 2020—again, the moment the Austin 101 line launched. Like my aforementioned speaking gigs, companies like Austin Craft Spirits would host tastings for locals or fly high-level tastemakers down to their facilities. Perhaps they would host a tent or table at an influential event to give out free samples. Unlike speaking gigs, though, you don't just need to see the product, but you need to smell, taste, and feel the product. We'd need some type of *Blade Runner*–level technology to have that on Zoom. Instead, innovative spirits and wine companies would ship the goods to the tasting party's locations, schedule the online party, and have everyone partake in the comfort of their pajamas. I attended a handful of conferences while sheltering in place—and while mingling and listening to people for days can be a pleasure, sitting in an office chair staring at a computer screen sounds questionable at best. However, the most memorable events pulled in the tactile with the virtual—the first day of the conference, we were surprised with a "swag bag" of conference material, T-shirts, and more arriving at our doorsteps. It was a financial investment, but the biggest investment was the innovative thinking that organizations had to do to serve their community when every other traditional way was impossible.

"A lot of errors happen when you try to speed up what's naturally going to happen," says writer Shane Parrish of Farnam Street. "The lack of patience changes the outcome."

If Austin Craft Spirits and other in-person-driven companies had been impatient with their business environment's sudden shelter in place, then they would have likely had three options: throw up their hands and close up shop; assume it will be over quickly (because they wanted it to be over quickly) and slowly watch their business atrophy; or flout the rules and have in-persons anyway. All approaches speak to a certain stubborn idealism, whether it is, respectively, "I don't want to change, so I'm taking the football and going home," "I don't want to change, therefore it isn't a big deal," and the most remarkable one, "I don't want to change, so the problem doesn't exist." It is remarkable because it takes an extraordinary amount of will to ignore a systemic shutdown. Safety and obstinacy aside, what these companies miss is the potential to survive well during the adaptation and even thrive after the chaos settles. As Parrish says, if you're too busy speeding through, you're not going to get the optimum outcome.

"[Our agility] allowed us to design novel product-tasting methods, increase our focus on store merchandising, and drive more online presence through social media and other tools such as virtual tastings," Godevais says. They went in with in-person tastings, bar branding strategies, and event bookings. As they came out of shelter in place, they had in-person tastings, bar branding strategies, strong merch, a bigger social media platform, *and* virtual tastings.

In having to let go of their sunk cost, Grant said it was beyond pure resource calculus. As we cling to our existential security, we tend to forget how adapting can actually augment what we already have, do, and feel. It is not a zero-sum game. What if the business environment is just encouraging you to be more, not less, of what you were before?

→

CHAPTER 8.

PIVOT BASED ON WORLDLY CIRCUMSTANCES

There are many reasons to embrace a new season in your life. It's just that when we're in it, it's not clear that we should do so. Change-management experts say all transitions are difficult, whether "good" or "bad," or whether it is by choice or by requirement. It is the reason why the average American multimillion lottery winner is broke within a few years, often worse off than they were before the winnings, and why people who divorce someone whom they consider an awful person still miss the bond.

"Each of us has an inner thermostat setting that determines how much love, success, and creativity we allow ourselves to enjoy," Gay Hendricks says in *The Big Leap*. "When we exceed our inner thermostat setting, we will often do something to sabotage ourselves, causing us to drop back into the old, familiar zone where we feel secure."

Hendricks calls this an "upper limit problem." We all feel it, as it is natural to miss the security of being in the same social circle, wrestling with the same problems, or even in the arms of an old lover, even though you've outgrown them. The real issue occurs when we aren't aware of how heavily those psychological shackles sit with us. We have to make some peace with the loss, even when we have a so-called win.

Many years ago, I was up for a prestigious journalism position. It was all dependent on a final interview with the entire publication board.

I was nervous. The problem was that I didn't realize *how* nervous. I began hyping myself up in the mirror the night before the interview. And I saw it: my hair was a little too long. How could I take on this role and be taken seriously if my hair was unkempt? It's late, and the local barbers are closed. I do have a razor, though. Before I know it, my head is covered in shaving cream and I'm doing my best Mr. Clean impression with a—I soon realize—dull razor. And I start seeing blood. It takes about an hour to hack all the hair off my head. I go to sleep with a handful of bandages on my scalp.

And that's how I enter the interview the next morning.

My head was still bleeding twelve hours later, so I couldn't clean up the scars. The board was not amused. And the role went to a person who hadn't hacked their hair in a nervous fit.

This is a Hendricks' upper-limit problem. I felt intimidated by the role. I was still quite young, it was early in my career, and I probably wasn't sure I was seasoned enough to lead. What would have helped? If I had recognized those feelings of inadequacy, acknowledged them, and expressed them to a trusted person or to myself in a journal.

Author Elizabeth Gilbert has one of my favorite TED Talks on the chaos of change. In short, she was a broke waitress and aspiring writer for years. Then she was the author of one of the best-selling books of the past two decades, *Eat, Pray, Love,* and suddenly became a rich creator. But why did she feel like a fraud equally in each situation?

> For most of your life, you live out your existence here in the middle of the chain of human experience where everything is normal and reassuring and regular, but failure catapults you abruptly way out over here into the blinding darkness of disappointment. Success catapults you just as abruptly but just as far way out over here into the equally blinding glare of fame and recognition and praise. And

one of these fates is objectively seen by the world as bad, and the other one is objectively seen by the world as good, but your subconscious is completely incapable of discerning the difference between bad and good. The only thing that it is capable of feeling is the absolute value of this emotional equation, the exact distance that you have been flung from yourself. And there's a real equal danger in both cases of getting lost out there in the hinterlands of the psyche.

She's talking about a sense of normality. That sense of normality, however, can't be found out *there*. As we talk about later in the systems chapters, your foundation can only be found within. In my case, there were dozens of opportunities after the razor incident that didn't come to fruition, and an equal number that fell in my lap. Money has been up, and money has been down. You are reading my twenty-sixth book, and a handful of the quarter before became best sellers, and an equal number—I am not kidding—have sold copies in the two to three digits. The only constant is me.

It gets messy when we assume that our next achievement will give us that peace of mind. So we wait. We put our eggs into our future happiness, forgoing any joy, abundance, or gratitude for now. It spoils us being in the present, recognizing the opportunities that we have in front of us that don't quite fit in the box of the future we expected for ourselves. The real disappointment, though, is if we're cursed enough to get what we have been fussing about for so long. You become a millionaire and realize that your life is more complicated—and your family still dysfunctional. You get a best seller and still find yourself wrestling with the writer's block you used to blame on not getting the recognition you deserved. You ruthlessly get the job title and understand the complications and stress that come with the role, questioning if the nice pay raise is even enough compensation.

I've been fortunate enough to see my books on the best-seller list, to have my company acquired when we owned the number-one app in the world, and to stand on the TED stage for one of my first public talks. I'm fortunate not just because of my experiences, but because I know what the other side of success feels like.

I share as much in my book *The Ultimate Bite-Sized Entrepreneur*, about the year I spent leading the number-one app in the world, Cuddlr, while being the primary caregiver of my wife's first son and mine.

The year of my life spent nurturing Cuddlr users, guiding leadership, and putting out fires ended as abruptly as it started. During that same year, good friends got married, close family went through big changes, and my firstborn went from baby to toddler. I'm thankful I was there for all of it, but what if I missed these moments in pursuit of the brass ring? Your rollercoaster ride will end. Your bestseller will eventually drop off the *New York Times* list, your album will be replaced by another new classic, and your *Forbes* cover will be off the newsstand in a month. You will have to look into the eyes of the people you love and, at worst, justify to yourself that your time in the spotlight was worth sacrificing your connection with them. The trick is that there is no ultimate justification, which becomes clearer as those accolades, no matter how high, inevitably fade into the past. For each decision you make, remember you will eventually have to come home.

"Home" is the system of the familiar, the stuff that doesn't change, the things you actively protect from transitioning. I knew that my baby and my wife were going to be there, no matter how much hate mail we got, how we got slammed in the press, or how many tech crashes we had to deal with every single day. It's not that I assumed they were always going to be there; like me, you likely have had your share of personal loss. It actually came from the opposite place: I valued every day with my wife, and I was honored to love and protect our child. I saw him change ever so slightly every single day. I knew our time was limited; therefore he and they were the priority. The cover stories, the quarter-million-strong community, and even the payday from my co-founders' and my selling the company would be second fiddle to my family. (As I share in *The Bite-Sized Entrepreneur*, "After my bank notification [for my part of the acquisition money having arrived], I vaguely remember talking about what I was going to make for dinner.")

Years later, I realize that those limitations—having to care for my son during the day, only spending so much of my Focus, Agility, Time, and Energy—the resources I identified later in my book *Build From Now*—on the startups, and not tying up my entire identity into being a founder—actually enabled the success. They didn't diminish it. Freelance journalist Jenni Gritters, primary caregiver of a toddler, said as much to me recently. "Here I was thinking that trying to parent and run a freelance business was setting me up to do less. But . . . it could be an opportunity to optimize." In a social media post, she said she cut her hours, and then saw an immediate, significant rise in her income. "Reducing my hours forced me to fire clients who couldn't meet my rates; eliminate procrastination; get super real on what work matters to me; punt anything that's not a priority (emails, calls, etc.); automate/batch tasks."

Systems absolutely play a role in staying centered, but just as important is knowing, respecting, and even embracing the boundaries to what you can do now. Launching Cuddlr would have been a completely different experience a year earlier, when my wife and I were just getting married, or five years earlier, when all my money was going into keeping an expensive apartment in San Francisco. Gritters might have kept those bum clients—my words, not hers!—done potentially unproductive all-nighters, and perhaps procrastinated more if she hadn't had her toddler as the priority. And Elizabeth Gilbert might have burned out after the *Eat, Pray, Love* success if she hadn't prioritized her first love—writing for writing's sake—and we wouldn't have had even better work from her, including one of my favorite books, *Big Magic: Creative Living Beyond Fear.*

Having clear priorities not only keeps you centered as opportunities shift your world but also when long-term goals require short-term sacrifice. In short, being centered gives you patience. *Disrupt Yourself* author Whitney Johnson talks about slingshots: career decisions that feel like lateral or even retrograde moves, but that eventually give you the momentum you need to propel yourself much farther than you could directly today. It could be a simple decision, like going back to school—a short-term expenditure of time and money—to get a better job. Some of the best slingshots can be the most deceptive, though. Like Gritters, my primary caregiver role forced me to optimize everything.

> After having my first kid . . . I launched two startups, did two TED talks and blossomed my career while being his primary caregiver. My years of working at odd hours and [insert chuckle here] "waiting to be inspired" to create were replaced by a stable, disciplined regiment. In an instant, my 60-hour work week was sliced down to 15 hours a week. I viewed myself as a marathon runner doing a daily, three-hour leg.

My slingshot is, well, now. As my kids, eight and five, head to school, my work week has now expanded from the 15 hours to about 30 hours on a good week. And yet the lessons remain. It still feels like I have double the time! And those habits and sacrifices made during the baby and toddler years are paying dividends now, even writing two books, doing a record number of (virtual) keynotes, a TED Talk, and launching my #BringYourWorth show during our pandemic year. The point isn't the productivity: the point is that the hard lessons and opportunity costs paid earlier ended up slingshotting me into a better future now. We can be too myopic to see the compound results of the pivot opportunities we have at the moment. Sometimes, all we can see is the short-term pain.

"Typically when the word *pivot* is applied to a business strategy shift, it is considered Plan B: changing directions to save a business from dwindling profits or a dismal forecast. Pivoting was a response to failing at Plan A, the original goal," Jenny Blake writes in *Pivot: The Only Move That Matters Is Your Next One.* "But when it comes to our careers, learning to pivot *is* Plan A. Pivoting, within our roles and throughout our careers, is the new normal."

In the book, Blake breaks down a five-step pivot method: plant, scan, pilot, launch, and lead. When I chatted with her, she compared it to a basketball player with the ball: plant your feet, scan for your teammates, think through your strategy, and then pass or shoot the ball. First, plant is determining your values and resources. Second, scan is looking at your knowledge and your network. Third, pilot is getting information and doing experiments, as we'll talk about later in chapter 12, Lean Into Steady Growth (Without Losing Your Shirt). Fourth, launch is knowing what you need to be ready to pivot and how you can recover if your start doesn't go as well as you like. Lastly, lead is taking the knowledge you've gotten from your shift and sharing it with others.

As other coaches and I note, we tend to go straight to the launch phase: Let's go! But we can forget to ground ourselves in our values (plant), do a temperature check of the environment (scan), or even test our ideas before we jump out the window (pilot). To paraphrase independent hip-hop artist advocate Wendy Day, most indie rappers fail because they don't have the proper team, the right capital, or the business strategy to break into the competitive music market, but they walk away believing they failed because of a lack of talent. You could be ideal for your next career opportunity; but if your foundation isn't solid, then even your perfect fit will likely pass you by.

➡

CHAPTER 9.

STRATEGIZE YOUR FIRST MOVE AND ULTIMATE GOALS

So where do you start? It's easy to get dizzy as you fly up to the 20,000-foot level to the height of your vision and back down to Earth to get work done. As an old saying goes, the giraffe doesn't minimize his view to relate to the turtle. In this case, we are the giraffe *and* the turtle: we have to get practical to actually begin.

The vertical visual of the two animals is powerful, but in my practice I've found that we are actually oscillating between two different points in time. It is what we have today, and who we are now, versus what we want to have tomorrow, and who we need to be to get there.

"If you are going to develop as a product or an idea, then you have to leave space for tomorrow," Group SJR CEO Alexander Jutkowitz told me. "What you are as an entrepreneur today isn't what you will be tomorrow, and neither will your product or your audience. We spend so much time focusing on our bootstrapping lives today, but it is equally important to work toward tomorrow and the audience you want. It is about reverse-engineering the outcome. If you become reductive too soon, you cut out your eventual audience."

The late leadership coach Stephen R. Covey called this the beginning and the end. "Begin with the End in Mind means to begin each day, task, or project with a clear vision of your desired direction and destination, and then continue by flexing your proactive muscles to make things happen," he wrote in the classic *7 Habits of Highly Effective People*.

This visualization works because we start "flexing" those muscles we need to accomplish what we want. For instance, if you want to be the founder of a startup with a hundred thousand customers (the end), then you can see you have to start with the first hundred customers, if not the first customer (the beginning). This goes parallel with your evolving values: you may want to be a successful traveling salesperson (the end), but start doing it in your hometown (the beginning) and realize you don't want to do it 24/7. Begin with the End in Mind also helps prevent what *Pivot* author Jenny Blake considers a mental red flag:

> Often the more stuck someone is, the more they tell me what is not working and what they don't want, even when I ask forward-looking questions such as "What does smashing success look like one year from now?" They might reply, "Well, I don't want to feel stuck. I don't like not having time to myself at the end of the day. I hate feeling so stressed out. I don't want to feel like that anymore." Although it seems like they are clear on some aspects of how to move forward, this information is not all that useful. These are shallow clues that don't build a life or a game plan.

A better approach is to focus on what you do want. Are you working for someone else, with someone else, or running your own show (and, frankly, answering to many customers as your bosses)? Is working from home working for you, do you need a commute to get into the right mindset, or is a coffee shop or shared space the perfect blend of social and silence? I love working home alone. My partner likes the ambient noise of the office. We're fortunate that we discovered this early, and designed our respective careers as a solopreneur and as a pediatrician accordingly. The recent pandemic has given many of us the opportunity to try working from home, to temporarily settle down into a virtual space, or to be in a less-crowded office. And now we're realizing our true values. What would have happened if this chaos had never arrived? Imagine all the gems, all the insights, and all the potentially fulfilling careers that would have passed us by.

Your values check should be a regular practice, though. Like an oil change, not like a once-in-a-century event.

After all, organizations change all the time. They do rebrandings. They get new C-suites. They shift based on norms and needs. But no company, no matter how culturally sound, will be CEO of *your* career. You are your own leadership team. It's one of the biggest advantages the side hustlers, solopreneurs, and non-traditional entrepreneurs I coach have before we even meet: they know the buck stops with them.

When it comes to the most supportive workplaces, organizational psychologist Adam Grant told me that he heard the word "family" way more than expected. "I actually felt a little off about it. I mean, I hoped we'd remove the dysfunction prevalent in most families [laughs]. What they mean, though, is experiencing the same sense of community and belonging here that you have in your family as well as the same level of care: someone will have my back because we're in the same place, and I can get into an argument with someone and still go out to dinner with them later."

And like family, even thoughtful companies will eventually expect you to move out of the house, keep up your end of any commitments, and may even consume you if you don't set clear boundaries and expectations. You are ultimately responsible for your own happiness.

Your first steps, then, shouldn't be too different from being CEO of your own career. John P. Kotter, Harvard Business School Konosuke Matsushita Professor of Leadership, Emeritus, explains eight phases of successful corporate change:

1. Establishing a Sense of Urgency
2. Forming a Powerful Guiding Coalition
3. Creating a Vision
4. Communicating the Vision
5. Empowering Others to Act on the Vision
6. Planning for and Creating Short-Term Wins
7. Consolidating Improvements and Producing Still More
8. Institutionalizing New Approaches

"The most general lesson to be learned from the more successful cases is that the change process goes through a series of phases that, in total, usually require a considerable length of time," Kotter writes. "Skipping steps creates only the illusion of speed and never produces a satisfying result."

Kotter's steps aren't too much different from Blake's five-step pivot (plant, scan, pilot, launch, and lead) or even the chapters throughout this book. I'd argue that your urgency is already established—otherwise, you wouldn't have picked up this book! And it's worth noting how the broad action Empowering Others to Act is halfway through Kotter's process. To paraphrase Blake, you need to plant your feet on the ground, scan the environment and test your ideas before you launch your next act and lead others in the new direction.

And, like Kotter and Blake, I've found in my practice that we are so excited or so scared about the prospect of change that we try to skip the steps. When a client tells me "I need to do it now! Otherwise, I'm going to change my mind and go back to my old stuff!" I remind them that they *can* do something now. They just don't need to do something large and they don't need to have results immediately.

Inc. magazine tech columnist Jason Aten has a wonderful theory about this: treat everything you pursue like a side hustle. Keep in mind that it doesn't mean you should just have a potpourri of side hustles to pay the bills—and we'll talk more about side-hustle strategies in part VI, Build Systems to Bulletproof Your Career. Rather, you should just view each revenue source as part of a bigger plan, including your day job:

> When something is your side project, you treat it differently than you do your day job. Mostly that's because it's usually something you do, *not because it's a job*, but because it's something you love. That's important because when you do something because you love it, it gets your best effort. You're willing to sacrifice and take risks and pour yourself into it. Of course, it's great if your side project makes money, but then there's always the risk that you start treating it like a job. Don't. The beautiful thing about having a side project is that it gives you an outlet for the urge to be doing something different. It gives you a place to direct your creative energy, which makes it easier to focus on the things you have to do.

Aten points to Tesla founder Elon Musk, Amazon founder Jeff Bezos, and other examples of busy people having a side-hustle mentality. "Sure, you can argue that billionaires like Musk and Bezos have an advantage here because they have enough money to be choosy, but I'd argue that it's their choice that made them so successful in the first place," he writes.

The advantages are threefold: less pressure, openness to experimenting, and willingness to learn. If your nine-to-five was just one way that you could move farther in your career, then you feel less pressure to conform to their norms, compromise your values to get ahead, or stay in a position where you've capped your growth. There is an openness to experimenting, as, with a side-hustle mentality, you are more willing to recognize that you do not always know the "right" way to proceed. And because you don't put expectations on yourself to have all the answers, it may make you more willing to learn from others around you. All advantages have one simple truth in common: you aren't sure it is going to work. So while organizations may talk "family" and such, you are well aware that your wisest options may be beyond the scope of the current company and will always have your resources prepared accordingly.

The side-hustle mentality also puts you in the position of being your own best marketer. What is a job interview but a 45-minute symbiotic marketing pitch? It goes well beyond your résumé, as, like any good side hustle, you'll have to answer three questions off the bat:

- Do people actually want this?
- How hard will this be to pull off?
- What would be required to get this to the right people?

When it comes to the potential or current job opportunity, is it actually serving something its potential customers want? Just like a side hustler building in the dark, organizations can be creating in a vacuum and not have a firm grip on the competition, the complementary businesses, and the needs of the consumer. If the company doesn't seem to be giving and, ideally, anticipating their customers' needs, then you may be setting yourself up for a frustrating tour of duty once you join.

It also requires self-honesty: How hard would this be to pull off? Qualifications come into play, of course, but how much emotional labor will it require for you to get the job done? When we interview for a job and get an inkling of an offer, our first inclination is to be flattered: they want me! The same thing happens when independents like myself get hard-earned business opportunities because, frankly, we receive an exponentially higher number of nos before we get any yesses. But we can be so thirsty for the acceptance, we can forget to ask ourselves if we *want* the opportunity anymore, now that it is available. Jobs can sound wonderful in theory. How does it feel as a nine-to-five, though? Could you see yourself burning out in a year or two? Where does it fit, in your bigger career goals?

Lastly, what would be required to get this to the right people? Don't underestimate the amount of hustle necessary to serve whom you want to serve. And while this absolutely applies to the side-hustle world—as you'll read later, figuring out how to get your product or service to the right people is as important as identifying the right people—it is even more relevant to the more traditional job setting. Why? To be frank, you aren't in control. You may recognize that you can reach 50 percent more of whom you want to serve by doing a specific action; but if you don't have buy-in from the marketing department, the supervisors, or the appropriate stakeholders, then your brilliant idea isn't happening. When my co-founders and I led my second startup, Cuddlr, we'd have a two-founder meeting nearly every morning (4 a.m. my time in California, noon U.K. time). Those meetings led to new app launches, swift business pivots, and even our fateful decision to sell our companies—all within the span of 30-minute-or-so conversations. I attribute much of our success to our agility. We bootstrapped—self-funded—the whole operation, and I know the results would have been different if we had had corporate or venture-capital backing, a board of directors, or other overseeing. Having resources can be fantastic! Just remember that when you say yes to an opportunity with a salary, a check for funding, or any other type of resources, you're also saying yes to filters, checkpoints, and levers that will lessen your ability to always move in the manner you see fit.

Before you commit, remember to keep the end in mind.

➔

IV.
CREATE YOUR
SECOND ACT

If you're considering a career change, but worried about taking a
step backward, remember this: It's better to lose the past two years of
progress than to waste the next twenty.

—Adam Grant

I've coached hundreds of side hustlers, solopreneurs, and internal innovators—intrepreneurs—doing work alongside their nine-to-five. And the most common first question is "When can I quit my day job?" It makes sense: your passion project gives you so much fulfillment. It may be that thing that you're happy to do well into the night. It makes time go by fast, even when you're being challenged by doing it—and often *because* you are being challenged to do better.

But that doesn't mean doing it more will exponentially increase your satisfaction. In fact, it can be the opposite.

In short, don't quit your day job.

Drop the fantasy of yelling "I quit," throwing the open briefcase full of papers out on the front steps, and hopping into your car to realize your dreams. There is no '80s-style success montage that plays showing your rise to the top. The only two things waiting for you are hard work and realization of once-held assumptions.

The biggest regret of the many entrepreneurs I've met isn't that they started full-time sooner. It's that they left their day job *too* early. Remember, this isn't telling someone you love how you feel, finally trying a restaurant that becomes your new favorite, or getting the discipline to start jogging regularly. You won't be mad at yourself for not going full-time before you're ready.

There are a few reasons for this.

Your day job financially provides what Silicon Valley calls "runway." Like a plane, the longer your runway, the more time you give for your new venture to take off. Mileage may vary, but a good runway starts at having six to nine monthly bills' worth of money stowed away. That size multiplies based on your responsibilities: a single twenty-something apartment-dweller in Boise, Idaho, will have much smaller needs than a fifty-something married family woman in Manhattan.

Back when I started as a young single guy, my basic runway could be covered by a handful of good magazine assignments. Today, when I start a new venture—and I've pivoted from journalist to author to entrepreneur to public speaker and coach—I need to expand those future needs for my wife, young kids, mortgage, and even my retirement that is now much closer than before. The required runway is much longer. We'll talk more about financial runways in part VI, Build Systems to Bulletproof Your Career.

Your runway goes beyond money. Legendary coach Seth Godin says his biggest challenge isn't money, but time. For him, taking on another project means spending the next five to ten years of his life to get it going. In 2021, he turned sixty. What he's talking about is opportunity cost—that resource runway will require sacrificing other options, whether they are simple, like packing a lunch instead of eating out for a month, or complex, like saying no to temporary happiness for later joy. It's why the decision to leap headfirst into a new job or pursuit is less desirable than slowly building the runway to a more stable future.

And promises can't pay your rent. People want to see you happy. Despite the much-discussed rancor and divisiveness common today, we all want to see other people shine. It means others may be excited—even motivated—by your passion and commit to ideas, opportunities, and commitments that their future self may not actually support.

I recently talked to an artist frustrated at this truth. A handful of folks were super-excited about the new product they were launching. As with many independents, this factors into what we decide to do next: Is there an audience for this? Do they want it? and Will they invest or pay for it? They launched the product. And, in their words, all the people who said they wanted it didn't, in fact, want it. They didn't buy it at all. As of this writing, they still haven't.

The opposite is true, though, too: you will have advocates, opportunities, and support from areas you don't expect. When I launched a passionate book, *Build From Now: How to Know Your Power, See Your Abundance & Nourish the World*, I had supporters actually question why I was doing it in the first place. I also, like the aforementioned frustrated artist, had creators I admire advocate for the book like nobody's business. But who was who only became clear after I committed to the book's launch date, finished the manuscript, and shipped it on time.

The trick is that you won't know how much wind will be at your back until after you take the leap. I've run many runways and have met many others who have done the same. This will be the truth, no matter how much you think you understand your next move. Accept it. This X factor is why you should be thoughtful in your runway, as you won't see the real picture until you're moving on the landing strip.

"The biggest problem facing young people is a lack of specificity. They are starting in the head with the vision and not the reality, because they don't have a whole lot of experience in the world," author Robert Greene told me. "In [my book] *The 33 Strategies of War*, Pick Your Battles Carefully (Strategy 8) means fitting your actions to what you have and not overstretching yourself. You know what you want to do in life; but instead of working from your head and taking notes, the idea is to start with the world you want to enter: the potential audience, their tastes, and what's missing. From the intense attention to details and focus on reality, you then form a venture—as opposed to the idea."

Second, if you opt to pivot into your next business move slowly, you don't have to worry about basics. If you are exploring a new field, then explore the industry, get educated as necessary, and even interview for potential positions or start your business. If you are looking to build a new business idea, then use your spare time to figure out the community you're serving, what systems you need to sustain it, and sharpen the skills you need to start.

Either way, you are the CEO of your career. Treat it like a side hustle.

Financial entrepreneur Ash Cash says, "Your job is your first investor. . . . It removes you from worrying about the basics: where you live, how you're going to eat. You gain that brain space back to be creative."

I love this: your day job isn't draining the life out of you. It isn't stopping you from being great. No matter how harsh, it is creating at least some stability that gives you the room to be great. Once you quit, that security—no matter how small—is gone. And so is your funding.

Many learning-forward organizations will match the educational money that employees invest in their careers. In other words, for every dollar I pay toward, say, getting my master's, my organization will do the same. Some—such as in the case of Google and other startups—will actually *pay* you to go to school. And since many companies tie education to rank and opportunity, an employee knows they will get a pay increase or be able to reach new jobs that bring in more money. In talking to corporate leaders, though, I found that only a fraction of their employees actually take advantage of these programs. You're not going to better yourself when your employer, who is already paying you, wants to pay you more to do it and you can take that education, that upskilling, that power with you, even if you part ways with the employer? Sounds silly, right? But we make a similar decision when we complain about our awful day job, the one that keeps, as my late grandmom would have said, a roof over our head, eager to hop into a new dynamic without honoring the one we're in now.

Your current job isn't perfect. Your next venture won't be perfect either. But your current paycheck is providing for you. And your next venture isn't structured yet. Honor the structure.

In *The Passive Writer: 5 Steps to Earning Money in Your Sleep*, Jeanette Hurt and I talked about the power and security within the side hustle:

> While you're working away to achieve that big project, be sure to build-in smaller, related projects that can bring in income while you're still waiting for the go-ahead. The classic adage "Do not quit your day job" applies here: Damon built his first entrepreneurial pursuit, the quote-capturing app So Quotable, while still focusing on journalism income, and didn't go full throttle into entrepreneurship until his second app, Cuddlr, became a major hit two years later; Jeanette leaned on freelance writing for years as she explored public speaking, ghostwriting, and recipe development, until those alternative sources organically grew into more of her annual income. Treat them like side hustles or experiments, so the worst problem you have is juggling two different income streams. Alternatively, if you leave your main source of income and bet it all on a potential income, then the worst case scenario is that you end up with no income.

This is what "Invest in yourself" means. Investment may bring visions of Shark Tank, equity discussions, and high-profile entrepreneurship. It also can feel like quitting now is the ultimate investment in yourself. "Invest in yourself" actually means maximizing the resources you have to make the next reality you want. If you are like the average American, you have a company investing a fixed amount into the organization of You every other Friday. Barring your getting fired or another sea-change event, that fixed amount will be there. I'm not sure where else in life you can get that kind of guarantee. And, as Ash Cash says, that psychological safety takes time to create when you start a new position or, especially, begin a new business venture.

Instead of quitting everything, consider the slow burn of creating your next secure path. Let's explore how.

CHAPTER 10.

MAKE YOUR NEXT CAREER MOVE

I met Adam Grant at the main TED Conference in Vancouver, British Columbia. If I remember correctly, the best-selling author, popular Wharton professor, and organizational psychologist was getting onstage that year with a powerful message about cultural insight and business development. Years before, though, he'd been just another nervous employee in the wrong damn job.

Here's what he told me:

Early in my career, I advocated for a guy to get hired, and he fell behind on big deadlines. I came in one day and the senior leader started screaming at him, threatening to fire him. I was very uncomfortable standing up to authority—like, I was sent to the principal's office in elementary school, found out I wasn't actually in trouble and still started crying—but I knew I had to say something. I picked a person I knew would have my back, the boss of my boss, and I told her about the terrible injustice, how I worried he would quit and that we'd be worse off because the work wouldn't get done.

She immediately dragged me down the hallway and into a dark room, which I figured out was the women's bathroom. It was the only place in the office that had no outside windows. She said that if I ever spoke out of turn again I would be fired.

Might be a sign to leave! Luckily, his contract was wrapping up soon after the bathroom incident. And no, he didn't choose to renew it.

It was in this that Grant found his calling—what is psychological safety in the workplace, and how can you create it? But there is another, equally important gem here: knowing when to leave. Grant, like all of us, probably saw subtle and not-so-subtle signs that his workplace was toxic for him (and, perhaps, others) well before he got yelled at in the loo. The challenge is that hindsight is 20/20. Of course, the now world-renowned psychologist can look back and hypothetically say, "Yes, this happened and that happened, and that was a precursor to this experience. That blowup in the bathroom wasn't an isolated incident, but the cumulative effect of a series of moments." To paraphrase Steve Jobs, we don't see the pattern when we're living it, but, when we look back, we can connect the dots and see a pattern in seemingly disconnected events. Looking back, everything seems so obvious.

But how do you know when to go when you're in it?

There are three ways you can plan and even *preplan* when to throw in the towel.

First, write down under what circumstances you're willing to quit. Here's the trick, though: you need to do this *before* you get to the point where you are considering leaving. Ideally, this happens before you even begin the job or venture. I learned this from respected coach and marketer Seth Godin, specifically in his book *The Dip: A Little Book that Teaches You When to Quit*. As I share in my own title, *The Ultimate Bite-Sized Entrepreneur*:

> To explain, Godin quotes ultramarathoner Dick Collins: "Decide before the race the conditions that will cause you to decide to stop and drop out. You don't want to be out there saying, 'Well, gee, my leg hurts, I'm a little dehydrated, I'm sleepy, I'm tired, and it's cold,

and it's windy . . .' and talk yourself into quitting." *If you're making a decision based on how you're feeling at that moment, then you will probably make the wrong decision.* You don't quit when the going gets rough. You quit when you know you've invested more than you'll get out of it. You need clear, measurable metrics to know when to give up on your big idea or business.

It may be as simple as writing down that you need to be home in time to have dinner with your family. That may not always be possible, but if that standard becomes untenable, then it could signal that you are sacrificing more than you're comfortable with in your role. Or it could be more abstract, like wanting to feel like your contributions are being valued by the organization. It's not as obvious as it seems: I've met some employees and creators who don't care about validation and acknowledgement from others. They quite literally just want to do the work. Others want the system to be viscerally different based on their actions. And still others want their compensation—in income, in perks, in rank—to steadily climb as they put more time in.

I'm squarely in the impact category: the subtitle of my previous book, *Build From Now*, was *How to Know Your Power, See Your Abundance & Nourish the World*. It's not how to work quietly, nor is it how to be rich. And I've ended projects and quit roles that were too low in their long-term impact, as well as those that were paying me handsomely. One high-paying negotiation fell apart at the eleventh hour because the contract didn't give me the opportunity to make the impact they seemed to promise I would make. What would have happened if I hadn't known my intention? I would have worked with the organization and likely withered on the vine.

Notice that it isn't about what the organization values: it is about what *you* value.

Unfortunately, we traditionally join organizations, adopt their values, and then question why we feel disillusioned. We assimilate into the overriding culture, forget the ideas that we held dear before the job, and then complain about why the workplace isn't as supportive as we would like. Our ideas, our metrics, and our "why"—as Simon Sinek would say—need to be established independently of the workplace in which we live. When I say "everything is a partnership" in my coaching practice, I mean that your true contribution happens when you know what you stand for and you create or join a community that matches the impact you want to make today. They aren't doing you a favor by hiring you, nor are they giving you unwarranted love and acceptance when you ace the job interview. You are interviewing them as much as they are interviewing you. It's like going on a date and just being grateful that you're getting time with the other person. It's not a one-way transaction. And if we are just happy to be accepted by an organization, then we are blind to whatever clues, warning signs, or blatant issues come up during the courting. It's not until later that all the issues seem to come out of nowhere: they are micromanaging our projects and won't leave us alone to do our work; they are muffling our impact and aren't giving us the trust needed to make a direct influence on the company; or they are shortchanging us on our compensation and tying our pay opportunities to idealistic or unrealistic metrics.

It's rare that this behavior comes out of nowhere. But you need to know your own ethics, values, and metrics to which to compare it. Otherwise, how else would you know?

Muting or losing your own passion could not only block you from tapping your full potential but also from being hired by organizations that actually want to hear your voice. On their hiring process, Patreon co-founder Jack Conte told me that they look for people with a strong "passion muscle." "When we interview a potential employee, we see if someone can get really excited about something. I like to ask about the last thing they were into and see if they get excited. In a recent interview, they had a side project they spent a year doing—like a textile—and they just lit up! People like that get pumped. Passion is a muscle you can point in a different direction. If they get excited about one thing, they can get excited about another cool thing, and that could be Patreon."

Second, if you are serious about leaving, then you have to know when the gap between your values and the company's values is too wide.

Married business partners Imran Chaudhri and Bethany Bongiorno were Apple royalty: Chaudhri joined Apple when he was twenty-one, around the time of Steve Jobs's triumphant return to the company he had founded, and worked directly with Jobs until the latter's death in 2011. Bongiorno project-managed the most innovative Apple projects and teamed up with Chaudhri to usher in the main operating systems for the iPhone, Mac, and other leading products. They fell in love and, together, left Apple at the end of 2016.

To recap, one of the most powerful couples at one of the most powerful companies in the world got up one day and walked out the door. Together.

They launched a tech company, Humane, but Chaudhri told me that their vision was clear even before the startup was born. "We knew our future wasn't at Apple. We knew we had a loud enough voice, a strong enough perspective, and collaboration between each other. We knew Apple was some place we came to develop as professionals, but that there was an afterlife beyond that. Knowing that is really important: understanding the next stage, even if you may not have an exact answer." This ties back to Godin: know the circumstances in which you will quit before you even start. If you're not used to thinking this way, then it may sound ruthless, like you already have one foot out the door when you begin. What it does, though, is to establish a clarity of values: this is a line I won't cross, this is a non-negotiable for me, this is what it would take for me to risk leaving this position. I liken it to a living marriage contract. Every single day, you wake up and ask, "Do I want to be with this person?" and—this is key—ask your partner to ask themselves the same question. And, like your job, considering your marriage daily is an active recommitment to a process that, unfortunately, is marketing itself as a binary one. You are married one day and—poof!—happily ever after. You ace the interview for your dream job and—bam!—you are set for life. But people change, cultures change, and, ironically, you are more likely to be blindsided by unhappiness and dissatisfaction and remorse when you aren't regularly paying attention to how you feel about the partnership.

The bigger the company, the harder it can be to remember that you are contributing to its success. And Chaudhri and Bongiorno were working for the mothership. (Seriously: Apple's one-mile circular UFO-inspired campus is called the mothership.) Most people believe that they either are the single factor making the business a success or are an insignificant cog in the machine. Both ideas are false. The ideas are equally dangerous. Instead, look at your tenure as a mutual exchange: you create within this structure, and this structure gives you a foundation. It is a partnership. In Chaudhri and Bongiorno's case, they knew their partnership was limited. How? By having a vision. They had the benefit of being in the same circle as the co-founder and CEO, making the compare and contrast a lot easier, but you can still get a good take on the workplace culture without literally knowing the leader.

If you are in the workplace, then you already know the leader. They permeate in the culture.

As I share in *The Ultimate Bite-Sized Entrepreneur*:

On paper, [Uber and Lyft] sound like similar companies, both employing everyday drivers to turn their own vehicles into ad hoc taxis. The identities couldn't be more different, though: Uber pushes the remote, cool personal limo feel, as it originally only utilized black cars, while Lyft represents the fun, collegiate experience, with its cars initially having big pink moustaches stuck on their bumpers. Talk about branding! I know many creatives that hate the word "branding," but that's what you are doing when you say you only work with small organizations, or your boutique caters to the working class, or your startup was created for hungry millennials, and so on. It is what separates you from them. And separating yourself is a lot easier when it comes from your own identity, as you don't have to work so hard to be authentic. I heard Uber co-founder Travis Kalanick speak at TED and there is no way you could see him and believe he created Lyft. The Uber brand is a representation of him, through and through. You neither I could recreate Uber, even with a billion dollars. Uber belongs only to Travis. People can compete, but they cannot replicate.

Signals of your company's values are all around you. Do they support extended maternity and paternity leave? Are emails, notifications, and other communications arriving 24 hours a day, and are you expected to respond? Do you feel comfortable sharing with your direct reports when you want to grow? Or would that be considered a threat to your job security?

These values are reflected equally, if not more accurately, in how you are taught to treat your customer. As the saying goes, if your date is rude to the waiter, then they're eventually not going to treat you well either.

"To all of us in the room, we knew it wasn't just about the money. Together, we had built a business that combined profits, passion, and purpose. And we knew that it wasn't just about building a business. It was about building a lifestyle that was about delivering happiness to everyone, including ourselves. . . ," wrote the late Zappos founder Tony Hsieh in his best seller *Delivering Happiness*. His customer-service-forward shoe website was acquired by Amazon for $1.2 billion. "At Zappos, we had collectively come up with our own set of ten core values. Those values bonded us together and were an important part of the path that led us to this moment."

It is worth noting that one of the biggest startup deals at the time happened when a company decided to make culture a priority alongside profits and passion. In fact, to finish Hsieh's trifecta, purpose may be the quickest predictor of the culture you will create in your business. I met him years ago, and we had a brief but honest conversation about company culture. The truth is that Hsieh was just as nonchalant, friendly, and service-focused as his company. Early on, Zappos committed to taking care of the customer in any way possible. In the most classic anecdote, a customer asked a Zappos representative about ordering a pizza—and the rep managed to facilitate the process, despite its having had absolutely nothing to do with buying the right shoes. I could see Hsieh himself being just as helpful to a stranger.

From the founder to the management, cultural DNA is embedded in each organization. Aside from executing your appointed job, your other job is to pay attention to the culture you are joining, and pay attention to sea changes in it, and temperature checks on it to determine if the culture is moving in the direction you want to go or not. The last point is crucial, as we often mistake a consistent culture for a static one. Swap one leader for another, experience an unexpected market change, or make a geographical change and see how quickly a culture can shift.

For Chaudhri and Bongiorno, the change happened when Steve Jobs died in 2011. Barring a few years, Jobs had been at the helm from Apple's 1976 launch to his last days. He had been so intertwined with the Apple brand that it was easy to assume that the company culture would remain the same even after his death. This wasn't as true as you may think.

"Steve's motivations and intentions were very clear: fighting for the customer, even if what was great for the customer may not have been best for our business model or company," Bongiorno told me. "After his leadership, trying to drive innovation, creativity, and motivation while having to fight for the customers ourselves was like trying to turn a giant ship. Every day I'm putting on all this armor . . . I realize I don't fit here anymore. It is about technical excellence and driving revenue, not really taking the time to think about the impact we're making."

Steve Jobs's departure had an indelible impact on Apple's culture, especially immediately after his death. I lived in San Francisco at the time and distinctly remember the entire Silicon Valley culture changing on the very day of his passing. Chaudhri was groomed by Jobs, and Bongiorno led his most important teams. Jobs may have tried to pass on a legacy, but his living guidance was gone forever. In their words, the single-point leadership became more scattered across the company. A literal death may not precipitate the death of your work culture. It may be a change in management, a shift in customers, or a new economic cycle. "When values change in a company, you either have to get on board or leave," Chaudhri says.

Lastly, before you pull the trigger on leaving, clarify the bigger impact you'd like to make. Can you find a way to fulfill your values within the organization? If you couldn't leave, what would have to change to make that happen? And what would be the ideal situation after this to check all your boxes?

The answer affects not only when you leave but also *how* you leave. For instance, when marketer Cory Turner founded the animal social-media app Dogly, she realized that her day job wasn't against her mission—it just didn't hit all her values at the time. She would do all-nighters to launch the app. Actually, it was more like all-dayers, as she just wouldn't go to sleep. "For the first year, my mom [Dogly co-founder Jane Turner] was in

Connecticut and I was in Shanghai. We also had a few people in New York. I was moonlighting while I had a full-time job running the ad business for Ogilvy across eighteen markets: handling Coke across Asia and Perrier in China. I was running Dogly early morning and late at night to catch America when it began and ended its day. It worked out kind of well, as it gave us a 24/7 team: When I was leaving [for the day], my mom was working, and vice versa. I can imagine the reactions to the emails at odd hours!"

She spent about nine months burning the candle at both ends before leaving Ogilvy to do Dogly full time. Turner told me the decision wasn't about having a bad career: it was about recognizing the expiration date on an opportunity. "I knew I wanted Dogly to be a success, so I had to jump into it. If you want to do something on the side, like a 'nice to have' or 'nice to do,' I could have done both careers. I had been with Ogilvy for five years—I could continue and go to the next level or do what I was super passionate about, take a leap of faith and create something that may be big down the road."

It can be one of the toughest decisions: leaving a decent job for something closer to your values. The difficulty comes in our not seeing the decision in the first place. If we go back to the shore-and-island analogy—the shore representing your safe but limited career, and the distant island your more realized, fulfilling career—then the decent job is your beach chair, cool breeze, and drink in hand. It's so damn comfortable! Going for more would be ungrateful, if not selfish. Someone else would kill to be in your position. Sarcasm aside, you have to ask yourself if *you* would kill to be in your position. It doesn't matter how much anybody else wants to be in your role. They've got their own shore and island to contend with. And sans your dependents, your career decisions have no direct impact on anyone but you.

Jack Conte, co-founder of the artist-funding platform Patreon, told me we get into the most trouble when we don't heed the call of a better opportunity. "A lot of the time we're just psychologically willing to settle for 'good,' as it is hard to part ways. As a CEO or leader, we're willing to let people go. As a creator, having a collaboration that kinda makes you happy, so you don't have time to take other collaborations, we often end up settling for something that is pretty good or OK, and not leaving room for fabulous. Sometimes you have to say goodbye to something good for something great."

There is multifaceted wisdom in Turner's approach. First, you should keep your day job as long as possible. She spent the first year burning the midnight oil to design her app, to get it to her desired audience, and then to turn the feedback into an improved app and start all over again. In Silicon Valley, we call this Eric Ries's Lean Startup cycle and the result the Minimal Viable Product (MVP). How much do you have to give your customer so they can let you know what they like, don't like, and whether they want it? As we talked about earlier, you can view your day job as your first investor. This is why side hustles are more powerful than quitting your day job: a steady flow of income buys you the time to create MVPs, whether it be a startup, researching jobs in a new field, or upskilling yourself for the next opportunity.

Second, you should observe not only when you want to quit but also when the next potential move won't be available anymore. As Turner said, she knew she had a hit—but only if she acted now. It can be instinctual, but our instincts can be backed by feedback, research, and data. Feedback is your community saying, "Yes, I want this!" Research is the broader market saying, "Yes, we need this!" And data is looking at your resources and saying, "Yes, this is possible!" For Dogly, the MVPs showed the demand for what the platform provided (feedback) as well as a good map of competitors and supporters (research). And the nine-month prep gave Turner an opportunity to save up her money, develop productivity systems, and otherwise prepare to become a full-time startup founder (data).

Write down under what circumstances you're willing to quit, quantify the gap between your values and the company's, and know what kind of impact you'd like to make *before* you leave the place. Otherwise, you're prepping yourself for a long time in the in-between. As *The 48 Laws of Power* author Robert Greene says, "Always plan to the very end."

➡

CHAPTER 11.

LEAN INTO STEADY GROWTH (WITHOUT LOSING YOUR SHIRT)

B ig risk, big reward. No pain, no gain. Go big or go home. In America, we've been indoctrinated into a culture of extremes. Having a little success or creating slow and steady growth doesn't fit the narrative. It isn't as celebrated as, say, the man who bet everything and lost it all ("He just went for it!") or the woman who risked her life for a now successful startup ("Oh, the dedication!"). But what if they weren't actually painted into a corner? What if they, even subconsciously, chose to be reckless? It's not as ridiculous as it sounds.

It's an easy trap to fall into: we have two choices and must absolutely go full throttle into one while leaving the other behind. We either stay in a job we hate or quit it to start our own business. We either get married and start a family or dedicate our lives to our careers. There is no flexibility. You're either all in or you give up. You must choose now.

I call it the fallacy of extremes. There are three big reasons why we fall into the fallacy of extremes: it forces us to take action; it makes us feel more dedicated; and it absolves us of the burden of having to decide at all. One, being forced to take action helps us run away from the fear and, unfortunately, the sensible details of our decision. The sensible approach is infinitely less romantic. Skydiving out of a plane is the most exciting prop-osition, but sometimes you'll see that the plane itself is heading toward the runway and you don't need to skydive at all. Two, we like the feeling of being more dedicated. It is a badge of honor. We want to show everyone—our colleagues, our social circles, ourselves—just how dedicated we are to a particular belief or concept, as that is our measure of success. We want the glory of saying, "I stayed up all night, every night, until my startup was a success," or, "I'm the first one in and the last one out at my job," or, "I am so busy, I didn't have enough time to eat lunch. I'm crushing it!" We all have lots of pressure, from creating financial stability to growing personal relationships. "Pressure" itself isn't enough reason to say that we have to make a particular choice. We should own our own decisions. Three, going to extremes absolves us of the burden of choice. We just get it over with. We constantly face tough choices as we create closer to Gay Hendricks's Zone of Genius. Some people feel like they have to constantly choose between meaningful entrepreneurial work and being present for their family or being mediocre at both—*and you do too*. The problem with this argument is that it falls prey to extremes: you can't just be a decent or pretty good parent, but you have to be an excellent parent, and if you can't be an excellent parent, then you will be mediocre, which means you should just focus on what's most important to you—the business. The reverse applies here as well. In reality, we could take five minutes to eat a meal for health, ten minutes for a quick nap for rest, or fifteen minutes to spend with our family to build relationships. But we choose not to. It's not because that is just how creative entrepreneurship is. It's because we choose to be that kind of entrepreneur.

Just own it.

"It's a very common story—it seems like there has to be some kind of great (and often self-inflicted) suffering before there can be success. But the answer is, no, not necessarily," science writer Kayt Sukel, author of *The Art of Risk: The New Science of Courage, Caution, and Chance*, told me. She spent years studying how our brains evaluate risk, why some of us will bet everything in Vegas and not go bungee jumping, and what it means to truly be a "risk-taker."

"Here's the thing: risk is not the same as impulsivity. The guy who quits his job on a long shot, and does so by the seat of his pants, probably isn't going to go anywhere but the homeless shelter."

A lack of preparation is sexy but not a recipe for any success. Even the most seemingly spontaneous successful experiences are cultivated in some form. For instance, Will Smith went from being one of the most popular actors in the world to barely selling tickets. He then leaned into social media, founded the marketing company Westbrook Media, and then strategically created spontaneous content. It worked not only to help revive his box-office attention but to sell everything else too.

"Will Smith posted a pic and said he's 'in the worst shape of his life.' Post goes viral," says Dan Runcie, founder of the music-marketing platform Trapital. "Two days later, Will Smith announced a new YouTube six-part docuseries about getting back in shape. This is Westbrook Media flywheel in action."

The flywheel concept is worth breaking down, but first we need to see that Smith's virality is as strategic as an advertising campaign. We think going viral is an accident—just the right idea at the right time. Usually, it is a blend of cultural trends and hard work disguised as overnight success. In Smith's case, the usually buff star—one of his last major roles was playing Muhammad Ali—posted a picture of himself with a big gut. The cultural trend was quarantine: he'd gotten out of shape during the 2020–2021 coronavirus shelter-in-place order, which many of us could relate to. The hard work was his established brand: Smith has spent three decades cultivating a talented yet approachable guy-next-door image. We didn't see the funny picture and feel sorry for the man: we looked at the picture and saw ourselves.

When my two co-founders and I launched Cuddlr in 2014, the unknown app from three unknown creators was immediately on every major late-night and morning talk show, featured in major online newspapers and magazines, and pulled in more than 100,000 users within the first week. Our app connected strangers for hugs and, according to the press, seemed to go viral out of nowhere. But it didn't. The cultural trend was hookup apps: interest in Tinder, Grindr, and other sex and dating apps was at an all-time high, but there were no platonic equivalents to them. The hard work was our strategic experience: I was a longtime journalist, so I knew how news broke and the best way to position our app for the media and had spent five years writing a book studying the connection between intimacy and technology. My co-founders knew programming and art, respectively, just as well as I knew my fields. Decades of dedication turned our app into an overnight success.

But to the uninitiated, onetime Hollywood heartthrob Will Smith posting a picture with his beer belly is a serious risk. Releasing a contro-versial app—as my partners and I did—could have felt like a reckless bet on our reputations. But we already knew what kind of impact we wanted to make and even had an inkling, before we even began, that our actions would make a splash in the marketplace.

"The folks who risk and end up ruling the day, most of the time, are not acting impulsively. They are not [adrenaline] addicts at all. They've done their homework," Sukel says. "But, from the outside, we don't see all this preparation and foundation setting. We only see the jump. That's why it's so easy to confuse the addict with the seasoned risk-taker."

The preparation and foundation argument parallels Jim Collins's con-cept of the flywheel. Featured in Collins's book *Good to Great: Why Some Companies Make the Leap . . . and Others Don't*, the flywheel is the practice of steady growth until success begets success:

> Picture a huge, heavy flywheel—a massive metal disk mounted horizon-tally on an axle, about 30 feet in diameter, 2 feet thick, and weighing about 5,000 pounds. Now imagine that your task is to get the flywheel

rotating on the axle as fast and long as possible. Pushing with great effort, you get the flywheel to inch forward, moving almost imperceptibly at first. . . . Then, at some point—breakthrough! The momentum of the thing kicks in in your favor, hurling the flywheel forward, turn after turn . . . whoosh! . . . its own heavy weight working for you. You're pushing no harder than during the first rotation, but the flywheel goes faster and faster. Each turn of the flywheel builds upon work done earlier, compounding your investment of effort. Now suppose someone came along and asked, "What was the one big push that caused this thing to go so fast?" You wouldn't be able to answer; it's just a nonsensical question. . . . No matter how dramatic the end result, the good-to-great transformations never happened in one fell swoop.

The flywheel matters because it isn't one specific risk—suddenly quitting your job, getting a brilliant business idea, or investing your retirement fund in a speculative startup—but a small series of risks. In fact, they can be so small that they don't feel like risks at all. As Peter Sims says in *Little Bets: How Breakthrough Ideas Emerge from Small Discoveries*, our most well-known creators, entrepreneurs, and businesspeople are successful because of their thoughtful, strategic, and small risks—even though many have the resources to go big. "Experimental innovators like [comedian Chris] Rock, [Google founders Sergey] Brin and [Larry] Page, [Amazon founder Jeff] Bezos, and Beethoven don't analyze new ideas too much too soon, try to hit narrow targets on unknown horizons, or put their hopes into one big bet. Instead of trying to develop elaborate plans to predict the success of their endeavors, they do things to discover what they should do. They have all attained extraordinary success by making a series of little bets."

As of right now, Brin, Page, and Bezos are some of the richest people in the world. And yet they are making their wisest decisions based on little experiments. It ties in to *Side Hustle* author Chris Guillebeau's Sell, Create,

Ship theory from earlier. We test the waters, see if people are interested in what we are offering, and then serve them specifically based on their needs, not just based on what we want to do.

I'm a big fan of systems. How do we take what we learn and create structures so those lessons become habit? Jim Collins has a like mindset, to the point where he began keeping track of how he spent his time. *Juliet's School of Possibilities: A Little Story About the Power of Priorities* author Laura Vanderkam advocates a similar approach—"'I don't have time' means 'It's not a priority,'" she writes. "We always have time for what matters to us."—but while she focuses on balance and time well spent, Collins wanted to know what motivated his work life. How much time did he spend doing things that got him really excited? When did he feel the most productive? He kept track of the hours, day in, day out.

He discovered that his best weeks, months, and, eventually, years broke down into three segments:

- 50 percent on new, intellectually creative work
- 30 percent on teaching or sharing knowledge
- 20 percent on necessary tasks

Collins is an independent founder, consultant, and teacher, so he can spend 50 percent of his time doing experimental work! Even if you have a traditional nine-to-five, though, you can still play with the percentages and reclaim your time after hours or even within your work day. If you have a traditional job and want to up your new, intellectually creative work, then you can volunteer to lead a new corporate project, create a subcommittee within an already established group, or research your job description and negotiate more time cultivating the experimental or underutilized expectations. And all of us have some agency over our after-hours schedule, which blends quite nicely. (If you are a primary caregiver like me, then your after-hours blend could be 50 percent doing fun reading and research in your field, 30 percent spending quality time with your dependents, and 20 percent handling the necessary errands and financial work to run the household.)

From a purely business standpoint, the 50/30/20 blend allows you to do small bets, contribute to others, and maintain your day job or other obligations. Half of your time is spent growing into your next role. You don't worry as much about being innovative because seeing what's coming becomes your primary function. What would your career look like if you spent a chunk of your time sharpening your vision and learning more to reach it? You always want to be swimming toward a higher level of understanding, if not a better role closer to the impact you want to make on the world. I've talked with so many talented creators, entrepreneurs, and leaders who have become frustrated because they don't know how to get from *here* to *there*. It often comes down to stretching your timeline for success, building a strong community with whom you want to serve before you start pitching, and making little bets rather than extreme actions (I call little bets "bite sized," hence *The Bite-Sized Entrepreneur*). By baking learning into your schedule, you can hit all three goals: creating wisdom over time; making slow, steady relationships; and being moderate and thoughtful with your choices.

A third of your time is sharing your mastery, which, as other coaches and I know, teaches you as much as it does the person you're coaching. Any knowledge you gain becomes solidified or reevaluated into a better idea. It also can serve as research. How does your view of the world hold up with those you teach? What is the best way to communicate with others so that they can actually hear you? In my case, I have a weekly newsletter at JoinDamon.me. I share coaching insights, new episodes of my #BringYourWorth show (www.youtube.com/browndamon), and exclusive content. It always has been completely free. A while back, I hit a career impasse: I wanted to create more for my community, but I had a ridiculous amount of ideas. I had no idea where to start. After some thought, I decided to do the simplest thing: ask the community what it wanted the most. I did a simple poll with four different options and sent it. I felt nervous and vulnerable about it, as, although I trust my community, I usually have a strong idea of what they want next and don't have to directly ask. To my surprise, I had a bunch of replies within the hour. They wanted an online self-directed boot camp based on my best-selling book *The Ultimate Bite-Sized Entrepreneur*. I quickly set up a preorder page—Chris Guillebeau style—and my newsletter readers signed up with credit card in hand. The boot camp launched a few weeks later. (You can learn more about the active, recurring boot camp at http://paylancing.teachable.com.)

Lastly, a fifth of your time is making sure your business stays on track. How much of your week is spent handling basic business tasks? This may be the brightest gem of the three because it forces you to rethink where you spend your resources. The pressure to use the equivalent of one day a week on important, yet nongrowth-oriented, work forces you to create systems to run the business without you.

It's worth revisiting Gay Hendricks's four zones:

In *The Big Leap*, Gay Hendricks breaks down four zones we all inhabit: the zone of incompetence, the zone of competence, the zone of excellence, and the zone of genius. In the zone of incompetence, we are doing something we are not skilled in. In the zone of competence, we are doing something efficiently, but realize that others are just as efficient and our skill set is average. In the zone of excellence, we are doing something with very high skill, usually based on our own dedication. Lastly, in the zone of genius, we are doing something that is natural, if not innate. In my interpretation, the zone of genius cannot be taught, only revealed.

By limiting the time spent doing basic work, you have to reconsider what zone you spend your time in. It makes sense to systematize your day, starting with the zone of incompetence and then the zone of competence. Your zone of excellence may pay the bills—in my case, a master's in Magazine Publishing guarantees that I can always get hired somewhere as an editor—and may take up most of this fifth of my time.

As you may have realized, that means up to half of your time—in new, innovative work—is spent leaning into, learning about, and expressing more of your zone of genius. Innovation on the job, in a startup, or within a consulting relationship takes time. By baking it into your schedule, you'll be able to keep priming the flywheel until it takes off and, eventually, ends up priming your career without any additional effort.

"There was no single defining action, no grand program, no one killer innovation, no solitary lucky break, no wrenching revolution," Collins writes. "Good to great comes about by a cumulative process—step by step, action by action, decision by decision, turn by turn of the flywheel—that adds up to sustained and spectacular results."

→

CHAPTER 12.

MEASURE YOUR RESULTS AND ADJUST AS NECESSARY

As you make your first moves, you'll notice that you have something you probably haven't had in a while: space. For some of us, it happened during the pandemic-induced shelter in place. The hurried, automated habits we'd held for years, if not decades, were uprooted. Most of the time, though, we get it when a career or life change puts everything on pause. Where is my routine? As the Talking Heads might say, this is not my beautiful life!

This is normal as we evolve. It is also uncomfortable. What helps is knowing that it comes after any career shift. That is, in fact, the only way you can actually prepare.

The in-between state is a hallmark of my coaching practice, as that is when things are the most malleable and when we can enact the most long-lasting change. I share as much in my books *The Bite-Sized Entrepreneur* and, in particular, *Build From Now*:

> Pivot author Jenny Blake talks about being in a "goo" state: the liminal, unclear moment between finishing one action and taking another one. In my Bite-Sized Entrepreneur framework, it is the "renewing" part of the renewing, pursuing, and doing creative cycle, as discussed in the Agility section. On her podcast, Blake and spiritualist Penney Peirce described

the "goo" state: "Penney equates the liminal space to the time when a caterpillar has created and entered the cocoon, but has not transitioned into a butterfly. It is the space in which we are given the chance to rest, reset, and recharge before moving into the next phase. It sounds lovely when put that way, so why do we often want to rush the process?" But to the caterpillar, stillness is death. Just as losing our inefficient routines, dissolving the toxic relationships sapping our Energy, and unloading our overbooked schedule feel like a loss of our identities.

It's no surprise that retirement—the ultimate break from routine—is ranked tenth on the list of life's most stressful events. "Among 5,422 individuals in the [ongoing Harvard School of Public Health U.S. Health and Retirement Study], those who had retired were 40 percent more likely to have had a heart attack or stroke than those who were still working. The increase was more pronounced during the first year after retirement and leveled off after that." Yikes! The explanation from the lead study author J. Robin Moon, though, is worth knowing. In their paper, Moon and her colleagues described retirement as a "life course transition involving environmental changes that reshape health behaviors, social interactions, and psychosocial stresses" that also brings shifts in identity and preferences. In other words, moving from work to no work comes with a boatload of other changes. "Our results suggest we may need to look at retirement as a process rather than an event," said Moon.

A process rather than an event. Your complex feelings, listlessness, and disorder are just a phase between here and there. So much pain comes from our forgetting that what we are experiencing right now isn't *forever*.

Ironically, one of the best practices comes from asking if what we were experiencing was forever. As I shared in *The Ultimate Bite-Sized Entrepreneur*, "Spirituality teacher Dr. Michael Bernard Beckwith asks this question: 'If this experience were to last forever, what quality would have to emerge for me to have peace of mind?' He adds, 'I may need some strength or something . . . name whatever quality. And what happens is your attention starts focusing on that quality rather than resisting the dark night, then the process is sped up. You move through it faster.'"

As we discussed earlier, the more we run with our emotions of fear, inadequacy, or faithlessness, the more likely it is that we will skip important steps. The term "rebound relationship" is commonplace for a reason: we're so eager to get out of the liminal space, we will jump into any old thing for security or, worse, not give our best to our next relationship because we still have so much bullshit we haven't processed from the previous one. Everything is a partnership, and that in-between space allows you to process, sit with, and perhaps grieve even the worst of previous career experiences.

To clients, I compare our careers to a river. It may be raging and teeming with life, or it could be stagnant and filled with moss. All rivers, though, will flow with the cycles of the four seasons. There will be times when they overflow with rainwater, melted snow, and other hydration. It is always a balance, though, and every river has a dry season when the sun beats down hard, the water mists out into the sky, and the riverbed becomes even more exposed. It feels naked.

Then the cycle continues, and the river fills again.

Our job isn't to fill up the riverbed: our job is to make sure the cycle continues.

And when we try to fill up our riverbed before the season comes, the only thing we can contribute is junk. Your riverbed fill could be those colleagues, supervisors, or responsibilities you outgrew a while ago—those that *you know* you outgrew, which is why you left them or were removed from them in the first place—and wanting to squeeze them back into your life. Your riverbed fill may be the on-the-job requirements you complained about for years that were once necessary for your survival at the organization but now have become habit, even if you allow yourself to forget their toxicity. Your riverbed fill might be the acceptance of those you love who recognize, as you recognize, that you're not happy with your path, and you may have said or shown as much in your recent interactions, but you try to tiptoe around the pachyderm in the room and squeeze back into the box they have for you—even though you know it is a lie.

Can you relate to this? I know I can! Nearly every damn time I want to make a major shift, I'll suddenly catch myself kneeling on the riverbank, polluting my own river. This analogy resonates with many of my clients, because we all find security in habit and routine. We invest 40-plus of the 168 hours a week into our jobs, not including our career development, equaling about a fourth of our entire lives. Calling your career shift a disruption is an understatement.

Instead of needing to fill your riverbed right away, how about you see what gems you find in the exposure? You may get clarity in the limbo that will help you recognize what you want to fill your next riverbed with. As many of us asked during the 2020 shelter in place, when is the next time the world will slow down enough for me to check my values, see my direction, and discover how I want to live my life? We can feel like there is never enough time. And when we have the time, we can feel nervous that we've got it.

Breathe. Trust your process. Everything stopped right now for a reason. The shit isn't random.

In the aforementioned Harvard Health retirement study, researchers found four key elements to a healthy transition:

- Forge a new social network
- Play
- Be creative
- Keep learning

You may or may not be going into retirement or in the silver age of your life, but this is incredibly relevant to all of us going through a career transition. In fact, the parallels to this very book are strong.

First, you absolutely need to create a new network. They are the scaffolding and fabric on which you will build your next act. "You don't just retire from a job—you retire from daily contact with friends and colleagues. Establishing a new social network is good for both mental and physical health," Harvard Medical School says of the retirement study. I would go even further: the axis isn't only building mental and physical health, but also building networks in your current job and outside of your job. As I share in the next section of this book, part V, Build Alliances as You Create Your Best Business Brand, "You need to develop both an internal network and an external network. You need one tied specifically to your job, career, or field, and one tied to the adjacent areas. This is not optional."

Play and creativity go hand in hand, as they reflect ease in letting the cycle continue. This relaxes us to the opportunities we missed when we were too busy to notice before. Imagine yelling at yourself that you have to figure out the next act now. Right now! How can you be healthy, proud, and strong under those circumstances? You also can't be innovative. I go deeper in *Bring Your Worth*:

> Our biggest ideas are as fragile as a Parisian croissant, and the pressure of projected success can make them crumble before we even have the opportunity to see what they will become. They are too abstract to handle the stress test. It is why we should create pilots, just simple, minimal viable products that can get our ideas out. It is why we should do side hustles, fun pursuits we do outside of our 9-to-5 during, as entrepreneur Chase Jarvis says, our 5-to-9. It is why we should build support networks, so we know there are other people trying to make something out of nothing.

And this ties directly to learning. We have to slow down enough to actually take in information, think about our beliefs, and rewire how we approach our behavior. As I shared in an early chapter, I believed for years that I could have soared to greater heights without having to slow down for my number-one priority: my family. It wasn't from a place of bitterness, but rather a wistful view of what could have been if I had had more freedom. Later, I was wise enough to realize that my family not only kept me grounded in the successes but also that *they slowed me down enough to learn.* I couldn't just run from media interview to media interview, stay on the road for weeks at a time, or bathe in the glow of being on the best-seller list. I'd be on the front cover of a publication with my team while I soiled my hands pureeing adult food for my toddler, triaged issues for the app as my partner and I stayed up nursing our son's head cold, and changed just as many dirty diapers on the day we had the number-one app in the world as I had the day before when no one knew who we were.

You need milestones on a road that, otherwise, has so many twists and turns that you may look up and realize you aren't where you planned on being. My speed bumps happened to be my family. Yours may be something different. Going from 0 to 100 all the time prevents you from actually digesting any of the scenery. Your in-between state gives you a reprieve from the grind, even when you are on the grind.

Business author Dan Heath talks about slowing down to gain wisdom in his book *Upstream: The Quest to Solve Problems Before They Happen.* As the subtitle says, the book is about building smart systems so you avoid issues before they occur. As we'll talk about more in part VI, Build Systems to Bulletproof Your Career, the challenge is that the smartest systems prevent "the word avoided"—that is, consequences we don't actually experience because we were wise in the first place. In my case, my grounded family life helped me avoid tricks, traps, and hazards

I didn't and still don't realize to this day. We often don't realize how thoughtful decisions or even forced detours protected us from peril—and are less likely to understand what actually went "right" in situations where we feel like it could have gone better, if not believing it turned out "wrong." "How can you measure success when it is defined by things *not* happening?" he asks.

In study after study, Heath found that systems with less desirable outcomes had a strong commonality: heroism. There were folks, identified as leaders, who would swoop in and fix things at the last minute. Things would be fine, until they weren't; and then people would dramatically make things right, until they weren't again. Of course, as Heath notes, heroes are only made when the system isn't working in the intended way. And instead of stopping to examine the riverbed, nearly every damn time they want to make a major shift the heroes suddenly catch themselves kneeling on the bank, polluting their own river.

"It's not that the day doesn't need saving sometimes, but we should be wary of this cycle of behavior," Heath writes. "The need for heroism is usually evidence of systems failure." We tend to get so fixated on getting things right (perfectionism), getting things over with (anxiousness), or avoiding anything messy (conflict avoidance) that we can't see the big picture of what we're even doing. Heath calls this "tunneling": becoming so narrowly focused that we become obsessed with going through the motions—even if our actions are no longer necessary, need to be revised, or may even be detrimental to our main purpose in the first place.

"How do you escape tunneling?" he asks in *Upstream*. "You need slack."

He, of course, doesn't mean the popular productivity app. Slack simply means time. It is putting a buffer in your deadlines so you can think about any revisions along the way. It is stretching your timeline to relieve some of the pressure. It is giving enough room for innovation that, Heath found in several studies, is directly proportional to the amount of room you give yourself to do so. "Hurry up and innovate" doesn't work. Now, if you want to do the same thing over again, then sure, run as fast as you can and don't be afraid of a little autopilot. However, if what you did before didn't get you the result you wanted, then you need to give room to actually process what happened before, get grounded on what you want to happen next, and strategize on how you can approach things differently this time around.

It comes down to respecting the time and the place you currently are at. Business coach Jenny Blake says she currently likes being at about 60 percent capacity—which allows "space for innovation." But what if she writes another book, gets a high-profile opportunity, or another shift requires her energy? She'll have the room to take advantage of it and go to, say, 90 percent. In my case, those two years while I led So Quotable and Cuddlr and raised my baby had me at 95—if not 100—percent capacity. I needed to be. But the years before? I was probably at 75 percent. Ditto for the year following the sale of Cuddlr. Those bookends represented a drying of the riverbed, a starting over, and a refreshing of the soul. It was hard to accept that I was no longer on the cover of the *Wall Street Journal*, managing a quarter-million-strong community, or negotiating our acquisition with potential suitors. The ego likes to be busy. But thankfully, I did eventually embrace the fact that the fertile season was over. I rested. And then I had a best-selling book and was suddenly in the spotlight again at my highest capacity.

As Heath says, it's hard to know what works based on the failures that didn't happen; but I'm confident there is a direct correlation between creating slack in my life and falling back into the cycle of innovation and success.

Military vet and *Can't Hurt Me: Master Your Mind and Defy the Odds* author David Goggins summarizes what many of us feel in these moments:

A lot of us out here are pushing real hard, but we're afraid to go to that dark side. In your mind, when you push real hard, you have this door in your mind. A lot of us don't want to open that door. Push open that door, you're in a tunnel, and it's a dark ass tunnel. And you can't see shit. But there's one thing about being in dark places: If you have the courage to stay in there long enough, your eyes will start to adjust to the darkness. . . . You have to be willing to go way into that darkness and find more of yourself.

Trust that the gems are sitting in the darkness for you. You just have to be still enough to pick them up.

➡

V.

BUILD ALLIANCES AS YOU CREATE YOUR BEST BUSINESS BRAND

Real wealth is not about money. Real wealth is not having to go to meetings, not having to spend time with jerks, not being locked into status games, not feeling like you have to say yes, not worrying about others claiming your time and energy. Real wealth is freedom.

—Rashad Bilal

Creating a powerful, versatile, supportive network comes down to one simple rule: never begin with an "ask." Media entrepreneur Sree Sreenivasan said this during a discussion many years ago. I luckily had been practicing it for a long time, but had yet to hear it articulated so simply and so brilliantly.

"You should never first contact someone with an ask."

You get a new contact request through your favorite social media platform. Moments after you accept, you get a message asking for you to connect them with *another* person in your network. You get an email from a stranger. They say "Hi" and spend the rest of the email explaining how you can help them. You still don't really know who they are. You meet someone randomly at a networking function. Before you can even sip your drink, they are telling you about what they are doing and asking how you can help them.

Rudeness aside, beginning your relationships—and they are relationships—with others this way is both unproductive and dishonest.

Believe it or not, these interactions happen to me at least once a week. But it wasn't always like this. As we discussed earlier, the closer you get to your zone of genius, the more people will recognize your power and will want to partner, connect, or even just be around you. Power isn't pushing people around, flashing your wealth, or showing a hierarchical title. It is a quiet centeredness that others recognize.

As I share in *Bring Your Worth*:

That's what happens when we see our true worth within the world: Everything seems new. It is like you found the cheat code, or in the climactic *Matrix* scene when Neo sees everything for what it truly is underneath the intimidating surface. There is a system in place, and it reacts to how you show up. On better days, I can feel, and almost see, the exchange between you and me, between one and another, as we are contributing to the flow of life, and responding to our declarations, and fulfilling, or not fulfilling, our needs from moment to moment. We are all attached, like some complex, infinite game of Cat's Cradle, with you determining what kind of world you want to live in.

There are two big reasons why this matters to your current and future relationships. One, again, the closer you get to your truth, the more you need to filter who comes into your circle. Two, the people who can truly help you the most are likely doing the same thing. As we used to say, "You need to come correct."

The perils of starting with an ask are many. First, let's say you reach out to someone with a request and they give it to you with no fuss. What happens when you want something else? Are you going to contact them again out of the blue? By starting with an ask, you are building what marketers call *transactional bonds* versus *relational bonds*:

> Transactional marketing refers to a type of marketing strategy that promotes a single "point of sale" transaction. It stresses increasing the overall quantity of individual sales over a period of time. Relationship marketing concentrates on building a deeper, stronger, and healthier connection with the customers, which results in customer loyalty, frequent interaction, and long-term engagement. It is all about building and maintaining long-term relationships with customers.

You can serve as many customers as quickly as you can, or you can cultivate a deeper relationship with fewer customers. The problem is that if you're focused on getting folks in and out (transactional), then you have less of an opportunity to get them to come back. Why should they? You made it clear that you were connecting with them for one reason, and that reason was fulfilled. And even if they had different intentions, your attitude toward them will set the pace for the dynamic. It's the difference between your neighborhood McDonald's and the Michelin-starred The French Laundry.

So, again, if you approach a stranger with an ask and they give it to you, what reason do they have to help you when you return for something else?

To be real, we will eventually have an ask in all our relationships. One of the best ways to interrupt the transactional cycle is to do what *Pivot* author Jenny Blake calls 20/20. (She calls them 30/30 in her popular book, but you'll understand my revision in a moment.) If someone reaches out to you with an ask or you are doing the same, set a 20/20 meeting: twenty minutes talking about what your focus is at the moment, and twenty minutes listening to what *their* focus is at the moment. Blake's version has 30 minutes/30 minutes. I've been doing it for years. It immediately cuts the one-way conversation, prevents one person from dominating the time, and eases up the power dynamics.

It also helps break up another pitfall in the "ask-first" approach: What happens if they have something better to give you? We can be so aggressive in getting what we need that we can miss sweeter opportunities. It reminds me of a *Seinfeld* episode. The oddball neighbor Kramer burned himself with an overly hot cup of coffee and now, in his lawyer's office with representatives from the coffee shop, they are negotiating a settlement. The coffee shop wants to offer him unlimited coffee and a substantial money amount. However, as they start to say it, Kramer interrupts them midsentence ("We'd like to give you a lifetime of unlimited coffee and—") and shouts, "I'll take it!" They never finished the sentence. Kramer's lawyer puts his face in his hands.

Like the sitcom example, I believe our inability to catch better opportunities comes from anxiousness. We want something from someone. We don't know if they are going to give it to us. On a deeper level, we're not always sure if we even deserve to receive it. And now we're in a potentially awkward conversation, expressing our needs that we're not sure are going to be honored, not sure even if we deserve them to be honored.

We want the shit over with. And if they do say yes to what we want, then we can be quick to end the communication for fear that they may change their mind.

The best way to approach networking is to view it less like a transaction and more like a conversation. What are you doing? What is your ultimate goal? What are your pain points? By treating it like an exploration, you are able to share your current challenges, express your desired outcome, and give room for the other person or people to give suggestions based on *their* resources. You don't know what they have! How can you know that what you're asking for is the best way they can help? There have been countless times when I've connected with other people and, after a conversation, they share that they have just become publisher of a book house, organizer of a conference looking for speakers, or an investor in a stealth (under-the-radar) startup. The commonality is that none of these opportunities were public knowledge. There was no way I could have come with an ask related to publishing a new book, speaking at their conference, or joining their startup, because I simply didn't know to ask. Instead, I came with an open mind and the intention of being mutually beneficial. The rest took care of itself. It is worth getting comfortable in this space.

The most insidious problem with the ask has to do only with you: Why should you offer something to a powerful person when you feel like you have nothing to give? This is based on a misconception. In business and in life, there are so many types of power: physical, emotional, financial. You are powerful in your own right. A colleague of mine was recently frustrated by a mentee. My colleague is a step or two ahead of them in their career and has been graciously giving them insight, strategies, and feedback—some of which they usually charge for by the hour. But the mentee would never offer connections, signal up the mentor's work, or back off their request for more. Most egregiously, after a year of support, they never once asked the mentor if *they* needed anything. Now the mentee seems selfish and may end up losing their mentor in the process.

When you ask from people in prominent power and don't offer to help people in power, then it reveals who you are well beyond selfishness. It devalues you and your resources, not only to the person in power but also to yourself. You may be financially broke, but you know the right way to get media attention. You may not be a celebrity, but you can strategically maneuver through the American tax code. You know *something*. That means you have something to give.

We see it every day. Back in 2018, socialite Kylie Jenner shared a brief social-media post criticizing Snapchat's new design (on February 21, 2018, she tweeted "sooo does anyone else not open Snapchat anymore? Or is it just me . . . ugh this is so sad"). By end of day, the message was shared and liked thousands of times. By the next day, Snapchat stock had dropped 6 percent. That tweet cost about $1.3 billion. Jenner's infamous Kardashian family may have money, but what people often marvel at is their *social wealth*. It is an entirely different kind of strength. Don't underestimate influence. You can have all the money in the world; but if people don't listen to or respect you, then your money has no real power. Social wealth has gotten me, as a broke creator, into the same room as billionaires, and social wealth is built by consistently committing to serving your community.

In another example, Black Girls Code is developing a pipeline of young women of color able to imagine, found, and, yes, program their own future startups. They are building the *wealth of independence*. It is a generation that won't have to be dependent on outside (and often overpriced) coders to make their entrepreneurial dreams real. Independence may be the most undervalued resource you've got. Picture the king on top of the hill. He may seem all-powerful, but he is beholden to his subjects, as otherwise they'll force a coup; and to the country's legacy, as he doesn't want to be the one to screw it up; and even to the power, as his decisions can literally determine life or death. Compare him to the humble neighborhood baker quietly learning his craft, not separated from his community, creating his legacy as he sees fit. That's the hidden perk of being a clerk in the mailroom, an artist yet to be well known, a business owner building community behind the scenes. You can maneuver in ways the big guys can't. It's one of the biggest threads when I have a 20/20 with a media mogul, industry titan, or major publisher—they respect how I have come up with a startup idea, pulled a team together, and released it shortly after; or recognized another potential partner, licensed my product, and then doubled our money with passive income. I own nearly all my intellectual property, so, to paraphrase a rap lyric, I am not signed to a record company; I am signed to me. *I am the manager.* The heads of the biggest media companies in the world don't even have that privilege of independence. Therefore, when we talk, they know I can pivot, start up, and create at a freedom and pace well beyond their capacity, and that may be the area where they can give me the ask. You probably have a special independence, too, though you may not recognize it—and therefore don't see the power you've got and don't know enough to offer it to others.

That's the energy you bring to your relationships: recognize that you have a certain power that is valuable to yourself and others. Again, it goes beyond rudeness to not offer things up. By not bringing your worth and showing your value in every conversation, you are setting yourself up to be another person asking for something for nothing. You need to set yourself up as a peer in power.

Unless you're comfortable just staying where you are now.

CHAPTER 13.

CREATE PARTNERSHIPS, BARTERSHIPS, AND CO-SIGNS

When I'm talking to new entrepreneurs starting their journey, folks jumping to a new business role, or someone discovering a newfound freedom, the first thing we discuss is independence. What it is and what it is not. And they often have made the sacrifice for their new pursuit for one simple reason:

"I was tired of answering to people."

Unfortunately, I tell them, you just signed up to answer to more people than ever before.

For the new entrepreneur, it is the customers who you want to support your product or service, as well as any investors who actually own part of your independent venture. For the new executive, it is the C-Suite that you report to, the people who report to you who expect you to have insight, and, if you're high enough, the board of directors filled with individuals who have their own agendas. And for the newly free, it is the responsibility of building your own network and honoring the people in it.

That last point—it is your responsibility to build your own network and honor the people in it—applies to literally all of us. It's just that we can be too ignorant to realize it.

Your day job is not your network. You may have the ability to get things done, like talking to Carol in Accounting to speed up a check or know from Harold that the president's executive assistant will let you in if you bring her coffee (two sugars, spot of cream). That isn't a network, though: that is a culture. It is not transferable. Few things are sadder than seeing someone be unexpectedly let go from their long-standing position and, as they clean out their office, realize that they haven't developed any relationships, partnerships, or barterships outside those walls. They have built their foundation on something that wasn't theirs to keep.

You need to develop both an internal network and an external network. You need one tied specifically to your job, career, or field, and one tied to the adjacent areas.

This is not optional.

"If you have a homogeneous network, you're in a perilous situation if your industry gets disrupted, and now you only know out-of-work people from that industry," wrote *Entrepreneur You* author Dorie Clark. "Additionally, you're more prone to groupthink if you're not exposed to diverse perspectives and points of view."

I experienced this firsthand during the 2009 recession. It was one of my most difficult years as a journalist, and an awful year for media in general: I had longtime editors who were let go asking me if I had any leads on journalism jobs. Fortunately, my Silicon Valley network of entrepreneurs, venture capitalists, and techies helped me think outside of the media bubble. Otherwise, it would have been the blind leading the blind.

Clark points to Harvard sociologist Robert Putnam and the two types of network power you need: bonding capital versus bridging capital. Bonding capital is relationships based on what you have in common. Bridging capital is relationships built across differences. As you may guess, it's much easier to build strong bonding capital and relatively weak bridging capital. That would be a mistake.

"Relationships with those like you may feel more natural, but it pays to push beyond your comfort zone," Clark writes. "Indeed, research shows that companies with more diverse boards enjoy better financial performance."

Diversity isn't just diverse genders, cultures, and creeds, but diversity of thought. In *The Ultimate Bite-Sized Entrepreneur*, I explain why this matters so much:

> Artists can often be bad businesspeople not because they are awful at math, but because they don't mingle with MBAs and accountants who could give them advice. It is easy to stay in the comfort zone and, as we get older, it gets harder to leave it.
>
> Connecting with different professionals becomes even more important after we get established. Early in our career, we are eager for leads, feedback and direction. As our work stabilizes, though, we think we already have the contacts we need and assume the work will continue to flow. It's not until we need the insight of an advertising specialist, or a media journalist, or another highly focused professional outside of our field that we realize how narrow our circle has become. You don't want to be facing a difficult business decision and have no one to give you an informed opinion on it.

By having a diverse, well-fed network on hand, you don't have to develop contacts on the spot when you need them—depending on people you don't already have a relationship with for an ask, as we talked about earlier. When I lived in Silicon Valley, my hodgepodge of techies, entrepreneurs, and artist friends would gather every week to drink, connect, and recap. It became a magnet, as regulars would inevitably have a friend in town or another colleague interested in coming through, and they too would stop by whenever possible. The diversity in people pushed our conversations beyond any discussions we could have had in a less public forum.

I left the Bay Area a decade ago, but I'm still connected to the valuable people I met there. And when I needed to secure my IP for my startup? My network gave me four trusted lawyers to call. When I was trying to program an app? At least two people who were connected to me gave me the going rates for professional programmers and, if I wanted to sharpen my own programming skills, literally handed me the best books they found. Keep in mind that I was only a writer when I met them in Silicon Valley. They were a valuable asset to my network before I even realized how they would support my next career move.

The secret power of networking isn't learning more about your craft: it is learning about other people's craft, and that actually makes you more insightful, strategic, and secure. Being genuinely interested in other people, then, is more than just being polite. It is a smart habit to learn more about areas beyond your field—and, at a minimum, build contacts based not on where you are, but where you want to go.

Your network power reflects three dimensions: partnerships, barter-ships, and co-signs.

Partnerships are the most common—and, perhaps, misused—term. They can bring images of multibillion-dollar corporations doing a strate-gic merger or a political alliance based on funding. It simply means com-mitting to an equal bond toward a common goal. Imagine two people tak-ing tenth-grade chemistry class—and failing. A hypothetical partnership could involve their meeting every afternoon right after school to study in the library. They might catch their blind spots, stay committed even when things are difficult, and be more likely to show up because skipping a ses-sion would let their partner down. I have a great partnership with fellow author Jeanette Hurt. We both began as newspaper reporters and became friends when we later started freelance writing. Since then, we have been accountability partners who share our intentions, frustrations, and wins. She's been a go-to editor for my independent book imprint—all my indie books have her thumbprint on them—just as I am her sounding board for all things public speaking, contract, and entrepreneurship-related. We even collaborated on the book *The Passive Writer: 5 Ways to Make Money in Your Sleep* and published it through my imprint. As with Hurt and me, I think the best partnerships work between complementary people: I'm strong with the innovative ideas and "what if?" questions, while she is fantastic at creative execution and strategic editing. She knows travel, food, and spirits like the back of her hand, just as I can talk non-traditional entrepreneurs, technology, and work–life integration all day. I found the same dynamic with my most successful startup, Cuddlr, with me knowing the media and culture, co-founder Charlie Williams having programming and startup expertise, and co-founder Jeff Kulak understanding art direction and design. Your partnerships might not benefit from overlapping skill sets, but you absolutely need a unified vision for what you want to accomplish.

Barterships mean trading an abundant resource of yours for an abundant resource of someone else's. There is no money exchanged. In fact, that's kind of the point. The power here is creating more without breaking the bank. For instance, longtime musician Purple Fluorite started his own independent music imprint around the time I began my entrepreneurship journey. When I started my own publishing imprint and the eponymous book *Bring Your Worth*, I asked Purple Fluorite to do the official theme song, "#BringYourWorth featuring Damon Brown." It was on his label. Shortly after, for the *Bring Your Worth* audiobook, I featured Purple Fluorite's music in the interludes. We exposed our unique audiences to each other, we played into our particular strengths—music versus content—and, as one or both products take off, we both get paid.

Co-signing is sharing your social capital to help someone be recognized in your circle. Co-signs are also free. It is you sharing your network. My favorite definition of co-signing? Your name being spoken in rooms that you don't usually have access to. This is a powerful, underestimated tool in networking. A common example would be a fellow author endorsing my book on the cover: someone considering my book will see her name on it, too, and if they are a fan of hers, then they are more likely to believe that they'll be a fan of mine. As social expert David Burkus named his latest book, networking is based on *A Friend of a Friend*. The influence can be way more subtle, though. For instance, a longtime journalism colleague and friend, Violet Blue, interviewed me as an expert for an article on Silicon Valley diversity (a co-sign from Blue). The piece went viral and caught the eye of the TED conference organizers, and they reached out to ask if I would attend the next event (a co-sign from TED). I went and loved the conference, joined the community, and encouraged others to get involved (a co-sign from me). And so on.

I have been a freelance writer for more than two decades, bootstrapped my two startups (which means no outside money), run my own private coaching practice by myself, and started my independent publishing imprint, which now has nine books. I *know* I thrive the most when I run the show! And even in my extreme independence, every single success under my belt included partnerships, barterships, and co-signs. If you're skeptical, reread the above section and see that each instance played a pivotal part in my career. Without my network, you wouldn't even be reading this book right now. You need other people. I don't care if you have a pile of money, several best sellers, and a strong name brand. I have two out of the three, but I suspect becoming incredibly rich won't change the strategy. It shouldn't change yours either.

When I asked *The 48 Laws of Power* author Robert Greene if our connections mattered more today in the social-media age than they did in the days of kings and queens, he responded quickly with a "No, not at all!" We have always needed people, and our reputation, opportunities, and power are tied directly to others, he says:

Take the court of Louis XIV, where lots of laws [featured in *The 48 Laws of Power*] were observed. It was a wide-open space, not unlike the Internet, but it was in Versailles, and there was no privacy—everyone heard about what you had for breakfast. The king would raise his eyebrow and look in your direction if he heard something strange coming from your mouth on the other side of the court—and people would stop and look in that direction at you. In fact, the public world was probably more intense then than it is now.

If bosses are paying attention to your tweets, you need to understand the dynamic. People don't understand that—putting info on Facebook or Twitter, putting all kinds of stuff on there that you wouldn't put on your résumé! Maybe do two different public pages: one for yourself and another for the rest of the world. You have control, and the naïve approach to life is to think, "I can do what I want, they will pay me well. . . ," but that's the stupid, naïve way. When you use this new technology, you can play with it—create a mask or make a character that is interesting.

He finishes with what we all need to remember: "Human nature is what it is—I don't care what happens with technology."

Nowhere is this tech challenge more apparent than the mutual intro. You meet someone new who you want to support and realize they could benefit from meeting someone else in your trusted circle. Great! In previous generations, and even in my much younger days, you couldn't just DM them or do an email chain. You would have to do a gentle courting of both parties, perhaps with literally a party: you'd tell one person that the other person is of interest, that you'll be having coffee/eating dinner/attending a party that they will likely attend, and maybe they should come through and say hi. A party or a bar may be the most common setup, as the crowds, food/drink/entertainment, and easy entrance (and easy exit) keep the pressure low. They both attend, you do a warm introduction, and, if things look OK, you see your own way out and let them talk. Amazingly, if I wanted two people to connect, this is how we did things well through grad school. You'd think the early aughts were a Jane Austen novel.

What never happened, though, was the cold intro. "Hey, it's been a while. I'm connecting you to Randy! He is an aspiring founder. He's cc'd on this message. Anyway, I told him that you were a founder and that you're super generous with sharing your wisdom. Happy to connect!" You don't know Randy, your so-called friend didn't check with you first, and now you have the responsibility to talk to Randy—an obligation, whether you are happy to talk to him or not, built on the threat of social shaming—or to tell Randy that you don't want to talk to him—which may trigger guilty feelings and even risk your relationship with the friend. Imagine a friend doing this in person and bringing their new friend Randy to your house unannounced! Technology makes this easier, but easier doesn't make it right. This approach is toxic and inconsiderate.

"I don't think social networks are all evil—we see lots of positive as well as negative, but I don't think they are the same thing as real-life connections," psychologist and *The Sweet Spot* author Christine Carter told me. "The more positive aspect is that they enable real-life connections to deepen, but it will never compensate for real-life connections. Yes, as we become more mobile, we can stay connected to people we met in our old neighborhood. Is it the same as having the close connection? No."

The healthy way to connect two people is to, first, mention the broad attributes of the other person: "I may know someone who can help. Let me check and see what I can do." This way, you don't promise that they will get involved and, depending on who you're talking to, they don't know the person's name to potentially look up online—a potential Pandora's box you do not want to open. Next, reach out to the other person: "I have someone who could use your insight/be a potential collaborator. Here's their website. Check it out and let me know if you'd like me to connect you two. Happy either way!" It lets the second person be in control of whether the connection happens. The approach is even more important when the first person is more likely to give the second person an ask. If the second person says no, then drop it for all parties. If the first person follows up, just let them know that your connection didn't pan out (it doesn't matter why, and they don't need to know why). However, if the second person says yes, then keep it simple: send an email to both of them saying you're excited to connect them, sharing an extremely short, one-or-two-sentence bio of each person with a web link as appropriate ("Randy, Damon is a . . .", then "And Damon, Randy is a . . ."), and then say "Enjoy chatting!" or something to make it clear that you're stepping out of the conversation. The rest is up to them.

And with any networking, your job isn't to remind them of how fruitful you or the connections you've made have been to them. A while ago, I grabbed a drink with an old colleague. A couple rounds in, they started telling me about all the support they had given to me early on and then reminding me of a good word they'd put in for me—unprompted—to a person of power. I'm sure my face soured. I excused myself shortly after and wouldn't make an effort to see them again until we ran into each other at an event years later. The relationship is still in repair, even though they probably don't know it. How can I trust someone who will pull out a proverbial abacus and count every "favor" they've done for me? A more critical question is why someone would flaunt their support, as it is usually rooted in deeper issues like jealousy, envy, and anger. If you harp on about how you have helped other people, then check your own issues and see if there are uncomfortable feelings underneath your preening. And if you are the recipient of such treatment, then be wary of networking with that person or group again—there will be strings attached.

If you still aren't sure about a partnership, bartership, or co-sign, then strip away the opportunity, be still, and just check in on how you feel. As I say in *Bring Your Worth*, "Sometimes others won't treat you at your true worth, often because they are holding more financial or veto power and abusing the imbalance. You need to build great partnerships not just based on the needs of the money or of the ego, but on how positive you feel working with the other. That positive feeling will naturally inspire creative, emotional, and potentially financial prosperity. Everything starts with a feeling. The energy from the feeling opens up the new opportunities."

➡

CHAPTER 14.

CONSCIOUSLY CULTIVATE TRUSTING ADVOCATES TO BRING INTO YOUR GAME PLAN

As a coach, I see a grave error committed in the workplace, time and time again: assuming we have enough power, vision, and resources to go it alone. Unfortunately, the more you know about a particular subject, field, or area, the more likely you will be believing your own hype. I don't mean confidence: if you don't recognize your own experience, then it is impossible to truly share your strength with others. Rather, I'm talking about arrogance. Whether quiet or loud, arrogance projects the thought that you don't need other people; you already have all the wisdom necessary. And if you do work with other people, you will make it clear, consciously or unconsciously, that you don't value their input.

While the first half of my career was dominated by solo endeavors, like being a freelance journalist or writing a book on my own, the second half has been collaborations. This was on purpose. I achieved some unexpected successes early, like publishing my dream project—the historical *Porn & Pong: How Grand Theft Auto, Tomb Raider and Other Sexy Games Changed Our Culture*—and having a surprise best seller—*Damon Brown's Simple Guide to the iPad*. And, ultimately, the reward was for my ego. "So, I achieved these goals. Now what?" I thought to myself. I realized the true reward was to use my platform to connect with others and share *their* story to bring about cultural change. It shifted from showing how much I know to leveraging my network to better serve the world.

There were two surprise "side effects." First, my output became prolific: I went from doing about a half-dozen books in a decade to a dozen and a half in the following decade. My books became co-authorships with SMEs (subject-matter experts), my articles became collaborations, and, more recently, my solopreneurships became co-founderships. And second, when I shared the proverbial wealth, my successes became even bigger. My single best seller was eclipsed by two more popular best sellers, the first a co-authorship and the second a collaboration with an editor and designer. My solopreneurship venture, So Quotable, became a stepping-stone for my founding partnership, Cuddlr, which went on to become the number-one app of 2014. As I mentioned in the previous section, Charlie Williams, Jeff Kulak, and I were an excellent trifecta for Cuddlr, as we were all SMEs in complementary areas. I believe we would never have achieved that level of success on our own. The same could be said for the well-selling co-authored books that we are all still getting royalties from to this day.

In *Give and Take: Why Helping Others Drives Our Success*, Adam Grant says "Givers' success creates value, rather than just claiming it . . . a ripple effect." He splits people into three groups: givers, takers, and matchers. In short, givers give into other people or groups and trust that the generosity will come back around; takers extract as much value from others as they can, often from fear that they won't get their "fair share"; and matchers will raise or lower themselves to others in the environment. Givers need to set clear boundaries, but otherwise they are the most likely to have the strongest networks because of their generous reputation. Takers may rise for a while, but their ruthless approach will likely burn bridges in their network or fill their network with other takers who wouldn't be eager to help them anyway. Matchers are relatively neutral and end up falling in either camp, based on their current environment and culture.

I've found that the more of a subject-matter expert you become, the bigger the danger of your isolating yourself from the additional resources you need. To use Grant's terminology, it's easy to become a taker. There's a wicked trap here.

In one of my first collaborations, I connected with an SME on a fairly obscure but important subject. The project was in my wheelhouse, so I brought them in, showed them the ropes, and shared my contacts. They were grateful and receptive to the opportunity. Once we started, though, our conversations started to change. They started to tell me that *they* were the expert, so this is how the project had to go. They even began to talk about the next project, and if I was even going to be involved with it in the future. We hadn't even gotten a good start on the current project! Our funders recognized the shift, especially since the first round of work reflected the SME's desire, not the needs of the people we wanted to serve. I played emissary and, luckily, my own reputation—social capital, as we say today—was valuable enough to convince the backers that we'd be OK. I was using my own credibility to protect the SME from being booted off the project. The SME, in turn, had already gotten access to my hard-earned social resources. I believed in the project's purpose and, after a long year or so, it was complete. So was my relationship with the SME.

And, as of this writing, the SME has never done another project again.

To be clear, I didn't do a scorched-earth campaign about them with my contacts. *They* did their own scorched-earth campaign with my contacts through their obstinate, arrogant behavior. In fact, I would go on to do many other projects with that same network, perhaps because they recognized how I had steered that tough mission without speaking poorly of my collaborator. And, unfortunately, my collaborator didn't recognize that it wasn't their network; they were getting access to *my* network, and their behavior would determine whether those weak links to them would become strong links later and enable them to do more work in the field.

"Networks deliver three unique advantages: private information, access to diverse skill sets, and power," writes Northwestern University professor Brian Uzzi, along with journalist Shannon Dunlap, in *Harvard Business Review*. Uzzi's groundbreaking research on networks helped form the basis for Grant's givers, takers, and matcher's theories. "Networks determine which ideas become breakthroughs, which new drugs are prescribed, which farmers cultivate pest-resistant crops, and which R&D engineers make the most high-impact discoveries."

Networks, not expertise, ultimately determine our success.

It's worth breaking down Uzzi's networking trifecta of private information, diverse skill sets, and power. First, private information has way more weight than public information. Do not believe that information is cheap because we have the Library of Alexandria—and exponentially more—available through our smartphones. If anything, it has made information more expensive. I would argue that we don't actually have more information today: what we have is more "noise," or more irrelevant data to swim through to find the good stuff. Worse, if you're making business decisions about what side hustle you should start or if you should invest in a particular part of your career, then you have access to the exact same information as my eight-year-old with a cell phone. Private information, though, is spread only within the networks you develop, and is ridiculously more valuable than the most powerful Google search. In a simple example, I heard a Silicon Valley rumor (my private network) in late 2009 that Steve Jobs was going to create a giant iPhone about the size of a tablet. I all but confirmed the rumor, assembled a small team, and planned on self-publishing a book that would be a guide to the new device. It was announced, my friends and I stood outside all night to be one of the first in San Francisco to get the iPad, and I stayed up two more nights writing *Damon Brown's Simple Guide to the iPad.* (Apple was notorious for not including any instructions, and I learned—also from my network—that they would be following suit here. My book would be a business opportunity and serve Apple customers who wanted guidance.) I published the book within a week, and it became an immediate best seller.

No network, no best seller.

"Private information, by contrast, is gathered from personal contacts who can offer something unique that cannot be found in the public domain, such as the release date of a new product, unpublished software code, or knowledge about what a particular interviewer looks for in candidates," Uzzi and Dunlap write. "[It] is more subjective than public information because usually it is not verified [independently]. Consequently, the value of your private information to others—and the value of others' private information to you—depends on how much trust exists in the network of relationships."

You can know a lot of people; but if you haven't built trust with them, then you might as well not even have a network. Here's a quick test: How many people know your dreams, your goals, and your intentions for the next five years, next year, or even next month? Whom do you trust to know? Does anyone know? It's not quantity, but quality. I have literally a handful of people, whom I call my brain trust, who love me and will hold me accountable because they want to see me win. That energy flows on to what psychologists would call "weak ties," or people I do not know as intimately, but we still support each other in our growth. As one philosopher said, "You wouldn't have to 'move in silence' if you surrounded yourself with people that want to see you win." That private information is useless, if not potentially toxic, if you are not surrounded by people you can trust, and that often is reflective of our not building up trust with other people. The ripple effect Grant talks about cuts both ways.

Second, access to diverse skill sets means you have more ways to accomplish your goals. From Uzzi and Dunlap: "While expertise has become more specialized during the past 15 years, organizational, product, and marketing issues have become more interdisciplinary, which means that individual success is tied to the ability to transcend natural skill limitations through others. Highly diverse network ties, therefore, can help you develop more complete, creative, and unbiased views of issues. And when you trade information or skills with people whose experiences differ from your own, you provide one another with unique, exceptionally valuable resources." If you were starting, say, a neighborhood dry cleaning business, then you might already be an expert at the art of laundering and, perhaps, know what it takes to start a service-industry business. But do you know how to buy or rent a storefront? What kind of insurance do you need? How do you do taxes in an often cash-oriented business? And how do you separate your personal accounts from your business accounts to minimize liability, protect your assets, and maximize tax opportunities? Few, if any, of us would have this proverbial Swiss Army knife of knowledge. And if you were that knowledgeable, some of those tools would be much sharper than others. (In my case, I learned Photoshop in grad school, but you don't see me designing my own independent book covers—Bec Loss of The Bec Effect does that. Same for my independent business-book editing, which has been handled by my longtime colleague Jeanette Hurt. I've been a professional editor for years, but, like a lawyer representing themselves, a writer editing their own work has a fool for a client.) This delusion that we can do it all is why we see brilliant products with awful press releases, excellent restaurants with misspellings riddling the menus, and smart ideas that obviously didn't consider anyone beyond the straight white male audience. I distinctly remember being in a Silicon Valley bar when the iPad was announced, and my female friends roasting the name because it reminded them of a feminine hygiene product. It was obvious who wasn't in the room during the Apple marketing meetings.

Lastly, your network concentrates your power rather than dispersing it. As I often share in my coaching practice, today's administrative assistant is tomorrow's publisher, and today's publisher can easily be tomorrow's freelancer. You actually don't know how much power a person or organization you are interacting with will have in the future, let alone how much power they have now. In this case, power specifically is the ability for another person or organization to position you to make a bigger impact. I could give dramatic soliloquies in front of my wife and kids (which, trust me, they do not want), but TED has offered me the stage to speak. Version Consulting founder Neha Tiwari may have been doing amazing producing on her own, but I was honored to have her direct my first speaker reel. As we talked about in chapter 14, Create Partnerships, Bartreships, and Co-Signs, "Co-signing is sharing social capital to help someone be recognized. It is sharing a network [and] your name being spoken in rooms that you don't usually have access to." Your networks have power because they are the door keys to rooms you don't even know exist. To be blunt, your actions or snubs toward people whom you think don't have relevant power will shut down career opportunities before you even recognize the loss, and you may never even know that you missed them. That's where having trust within your network really comes to bear. When it comes to new ideas, Grant and his research team found that people considered givers—that is, genuinely interested in contributing to the well-being of others, regardless of their upside—were given a more open-minded approach by their colleagues and people in power, while takers—only contributing when there was a clear upside for them, even to the detriment of others involved—were often blocked by the very same people for even the most mundane suggestions or opportunities.

Grant's study results argue that the generous are given way more latitude by people in power—which, to me, *is* power—while the stingy are given less latitude by others. It's almost like a bank account, and that goodwill has created a cushion that generous people can lean on when they are vying for a promotion, pushing for a risky strategy, or asking potential customers to support their product.

My view is that being generous gives us what we ultimately desire: freedom. Ironically, freedom cannot be achieved without others.

→

CHAPTER 15.

STRATEGIZE WITH OTHERS TO MAKE THE BIGGEST IMPACT

T he best way to build allies is to tie your network less to your identity and more to your mission. "Getting rich" isn't a mission, but "Making sure every child over five can read" is. If you don't have your foundation set, then you can't show up right for others; and if you can't show up right, then your network won't reflect the strengths you need to accomplish bigger goals. A strong foundation will help you avoid what professor Brian Uzzi and writer Shannon Dunlap consider two strong network blocks: the self-similarity principle and the proximity principle. "The self-similarity principle states that, when you make network contacts, you tend to choose people who resemble you in terms of experience, training, worldview, and so on," they write in the *Harvard Business Review*. "Another obstacle to diversity in networks is the proximity principle, which holds that workers prefer to populate their networks with the people they spend the most time with, such as colleagues in their department." As we discussed earlier, the reason why artists are generally bad with money and lawyers are generally good with money isn't because of math ability, but because lawyers are more likely to have CPAs in their circle.

The diversity of your network isn't key just to your survival, but to your innovation. I know it is essential to my own career growth: I married a pediatrician, lived in two dozen parts of America, and studied technology as well as understood liberal arts. Being in the room with billionaires, brilliant folks below the poverty line, and everyone in between can quickly help you see how narrow your views—and your network—really are. The secret? Curiosity without judgment. We often will stop at our innate curiosity ("I've always wondered how this works!"), which is limited to our worldview. I am a South Jersey kid raised in the Midwest, so I wasn't curious about how a Moroccan loom worked or why the Tokyo trains always stopped at midnight because I didn't know to ask until I saw them in person. Educator Marian Wright Edelman famously said, "You can't be what you can't see," and you also can't be curious about what you don't know exists. The easiest approach may be cross-pollination: How can being genuinely curious about this act, this culture, and this moment help me give honor and empathy to others while understanding how their view will help me better serve those in my community?

In *Build From Now*, I share how this cross-pollination was key to one of the most successful companies—and entrepreneurs—of our generation:

Apple reflects not only the tech ambitions of the late co-founder Steve Jobs, but his Time doing transcendental meditation, his Time studying history, and his sixties' counterculture aesthetic. The groundbreaking fonts available on the first Apple computers? According to *Becoming Steve Jobs*, they were inspired by a calligraphy class he took in college. Outside influences gave him success in his main field.

"When I worked on Wall Street, my professional circle was initially limited to other folks in the financial services sector: bankers, traders, analysts, economists. Taken together, all of us establish a 'consensus' view on the markets," says Wall Street veteran Kabir Sehgal in *Harvard Business*

Review. (Sehgal, as we'll learn later, is a consummate side hustler.) "And most of my asset manager clients were looking for something different: 'Give me a contrarian perspective.' In other words, they didn't want to hear the groupthink. I took this as marching orders to tap my Rolodex for people who could provide my clients a differentiated perspective."

Uzzi and Dunlap write that the best way to diversify our network and our perspectives is to follow what's called the shared-activities principle. In short, connect based on mission, not based on status. "Potent networks are not forged through casual interactions, but through relatively high-stakes activities that connect you with diverse others," they say, giving Microsoft co-founder Bill Gates's connection to IBM executive John Akers as an example. Akers gave Gates his big break, ushering in Microsoft as the de facto IBM operating system in the late 1970s. "Schmoozing didn't connect [Gates to Akers]; rather, their trust, exchange of private information, and access to each other's diverse skills were by-products of their work on the same nonprofit board—a shared activity. Any executive can participate in and benefit from a variety of shared activities, including sports teams, community-service ventures, interdepartmental initiatives, voluntary associations, for-profit boards, cross-functional teams, and charitable foundations."

So, no, following your passion won't guarantee you financial rewards or any other metric of success. But it will allow you to do three things: have clarity in your actions, find the others who also care about your bigger mission, and build allies and insights that will help you accomplish it together. What I love about Uzzi and Dunlap's argument, despite being very corporate-focused, is that it has absolutely nothing to do with rank. Notice that there's no mention of superiors or how you should talk to your subordinates, and they specifically downplay the idea of "schmoozing." (The latter makes me think of hapless sitcom idiots Jack Tripper and Larry Dallas trying to get a date on the '70s show *Three's Company*. No, you don't want to be those guys.) Instead, you attract the right people based on your actions, and your actions are a reflection of your intentions. If the elements of a strong network are private information, diverse skill sets, and power—with private information being the most important—then your biggest allies could be in the boardroom or in the mailroom.

You are better off drawing people in with your intention, as I share in *Bring Your Worth*:

> The advocates will come. But first, you need to start. You want your purpose to be as transparent as a drop of water: Only take a sip, and you are completely understood. You don't need anything deep or heavy, any dramatic pronouncements. Marcus Aurelius said that your truth should be clear as soon as you step into a room, like a smelly goat. That strength is undeniable by the many, even by your detractors, and it is unattainable by the masses, even by the envious. It is pure and unyielding. Once you uncover it, then it can no longer remain buried. This is a gift and a curse, as you cannot unknow it, either, and you will have to do something with it for the rest of your life. Other people will recognize it, too, and those who care about you will dog you to fulfill it, while even those who just met you will know when you are in alignment with it. They will see it in your eyes. Do you ever look at someone and know they are living their truth? It could be ugly, it could be disagreeable, but it always means something higher than just muddling through life. They light up. It is undeniable. It is understood without saying a word.

It represents what business veteran Nilofer Merchant calls "signaling and surfacing." Signaling is showing your values in your actions. Surfacing is when the others who share your values recognize your signals and join as allies. "Signaling and surfacing thus brought a disparate group of individuals together into an organized whole," she writes in *The Power of Onlyness: Make Your Wild Ideas Mighty Enough to Dent the World.* "It is as if you look at the night sky to see many stars, but no pattern. And then, someone comes by to show you the orderly arrangement of the Little Dipper. Once it is visible to you, it's visible. . . . Signaling and seeking between people is the invisible cord of meaning lassoing people together into an organized whole."

A key element here is your allies being committed to the unified values, not committed to *you*. Seth Godin is a generous person, and I was privileged enough to work with him in his The Marketing Seminar course; but I listen to his *Akimbo* podcast, read all his books, and follow his work because I believe entrepreneurship should be available to all—just like he does. Brené Brown quotes pepper my work, my keynote speeches, and even my coaching conversations not because of her niche celebrity status, but because her emotional intelligence research so resonates with who I am and the impact I'm trying to make too. In my own signaling, I try to separate the ego from the mission. Yes, I want to make a great financial living and be well read when it comes to supporting the non-traditional entrepreneur. But the first half of that statement is my *business*, while the second half of that statement is my *mission*. That mission lives on without me—at least I hope it does, as not only will I die one day but I also recognize that I can't do it alone.

Separating self from mission has a serious upside: you are more likely to see allies than competition. Some of my coaching clients have actually become coaches themselves. (As a recent sarcastic meme says, the only thing a good coach can do is to convince their client that they should be a coach too.) And my work has been quoted—OK, plagiarized—in ways I did not intend. Ironically, in the latter case, I had people on social media disparaging the writer who did so, tagging me in the posts, and even linking to my original work and sharing it with their audiences. I didn't have to attack competitors, as my allies, many of whom I didn't even know existed until they "surfaced," ended up protecting my work for me. This perspective allows you to be more generous; and in that generosity you give fuel for other people to help finish the mission.

A glorious side effect is that the more your allies are tied to the mission rather than to you, the more likely they are willing to have you lead. It gets back to what we discussed earlier: the message is more important than the medium. If you noticed with Godin, I followed him with his books decades ago, then followed him with his podcast a few years ago, and most recently followed him into his online seminar over the past year. It didn't matter *how* he was serving. What mattered was *what* he was serving. And that's because Godin hasn't made it about him. In fact, as he is quick to acknowledge, it is about *us*.

Merchant writes that this is key to building a strong network that, as we discussed before, actually unlocks our freedom. "How you actually do the signaling matters . . . not by making the idea only about [yourself] but by presenting the idea in such a way that others could stake their personal claim to it. The former is a tight fist wrapped around an idea, the latter an open palm holding the idea so it enables others to pick it up and hold it as if it were their own. This stance allows for people to co-own the idea, which is central to onlyness."

We do not walk alone. The group defines us—as Merchant writes, the word "individual" is the smallest number of a group—and so our identity is always tied and defined by the greater.

When I talked with Merchant, she told me this tie between our individuality and the group is crucial to what theorists call "psychological safety":

> There is a reason why we give up on our ideas, and it's not because we don't have courage or confidence. We cannot claim our own original ideas until we belong to a group of people where we feel safe enough to have those ideas. I'm almost fifty, and for years I've been

going to conferences and have been told the same thing: Show more grit, have more confidence, and be bold with your ideas. I'd do that the next day and it wouldn't change anything! Until you have a group of people who can back you personally and give you a safe enough space to explore your ideas, you can never take the psychological risk to pursue your ideas.

Allies, then, aren't some folks who buy your product, share your work, or champion you behind closed doors: they are the people who allow your voice to speak a little bit louder. Without them, you may not feel safe enough to bloom as big as you could be.

"[Researcher Amy] Edmondson characterizes psychological safety as an environment of mutual trust and respect, where people feel safe to take risks, safe to admit their failures, and safe to fully express themselves," says *Leading from Anywhere: The Essential Guide to Managing Remote Teams* and *A Friend of a Friend* author David Burkus. In short, Edmondson's management study found that a lack of psychological safety made team members less likely to speak up when something goes wrong. "[Over time, it is worth building] that climate of mutual trust and respect. And over time that climate creates a culture of psychological safety. And that culture of psychological safety will create a team that does its best work ever," Burkus writes.

And everyone has a team—even you. In fact, that may be our biggest blind spot: failing to recognize that we have a team outside of some predesignated co-workers, sports setting, or another often artificial—as in non-organic—bond. They are your colleagues, your supervisors, your mentors, and your mentees, and perhaps even your family and close friends. I don't have any employees and don't have any supervisors, but I still have a team of supporters, advocates, and co-creators. In fact, any ally who works with you in some way on your shared mission is a co-conspirator—literally another person conspiring with you to make a particular impact. Without psychological safety, your team won't give you good private information, share their best skills with you, or bring their power to bear in helping you do your mission. "Yes-men" will "yes" you until you get out of their face—and likely head in the wrong direction based on their "input." (I'm not a big fan of scare quotes, but rarely have they felt more appropriate.)

Edmondson's work suggests four ways to create psychological safety for your team: viewing conflict as collaboration; embracing failures; encouraging dissent; and fostering civility. There are two types of conflict: person-based, and task-focused. "There is no place for person-oriented conflict on a high-performing team. But task-focused conflict, on the other hand, is a positive," Burkus notes. "Task-focused conflict, if it's seen as collaboration, is a great way to harness diverse perspectives, knowledge, skill sets, and experience." If you're having a tough time differentiating, think about the classic Brené Brown quote: "There is a difference between saying, 'I screwed up' and, 'I *am* a screwup.' The former, a task-focused approach, can be the first step toward a resolution. The latter, a person-based approach, is practically damnation." If you don't get honest, helpful guidance from your co-conspirators, then you should think about how you respond to their input.

Along those same lines, embracing failures gives you the permission to be wrong—and extends that same permission to others who may be eager to give you interesting feedback or data that may not be 100 percent certain. It goes back to the Carol Dweck extreme mindset theory we discussed in the introduction, The Noble Pig: an idea is either perfect or it is worthless; and if it isn't perfect, then I'm not going to share it. You can imagine how many opportunities would end up on the cutting-room floor if the people in your circles wouldn't feel comfortable coming to you with potentially radical ideas. The same sentiment applies to the last two recommendations of encouraging dissent and fostering civility.

"When someone on a team disagrees with you, it doesn't make you less of a leader," Burkus says. "It really means you're facing two opportune situations. Either you've got an opportunity to see another perspective, or you have the opportunity to explain your perspective and instruct your team. In fact, many times both situations are happening at the same time. But if everyone on your team is always in agreement, it means you're facing two dangerous situations. Either you've got a team where few people think creatively, or you've got a team where everyone is afraid to speak up. And yes, many times both situations are happening at the same time. Ask yourself, 'When was the last time someone on the team spoke up and disagreed with me?' and if it's been too long, then encourage more dissent."

What is the point in fighting for your point of view, sacrificing your time and energy, and creating champions for your mission if all you're creating is a community of people who won't challenge you to greater heights? So many times I've shared my favorite quote from award-winning filmmaker Ava DuVernay: "My truth is I don't want a chair at the table. Or even three or even half anymore. I want the table rebuilt. In my likeness. And in the likeness of others long forced out of the room." Your network should be the people sitting at that table. And you have to ask yourself, "How many people have I forced out the room?"

→

BUILD SYSTEMS TO BULLETPROOF YOUR CAREER

"If we're always trying to get approval from either our family system or our work system or societal system, then we're going to have to betray ourselves."

—Chani Nicholas

A fish doesn't know it is in water—well, until it isn't in water, and then it understands water *really* quickly. Systems are the water in which we swim. The problem is that we don't recognize the systems in which we function until they break down, and even then we may blame ourselves rather than recognize that the framework itself isn't working.

It's why we need some type of objectivity to the work we do. In a *Harvard Business Review* article, best-selling author Kabir Sehgal argues that you should have at least two careers. "When you work different jobs, you can identify where ideas interact— and more significantly, where they *should* interact," says the writer, Fortune 500 corporate strategist, U.S. Navy veteran, and multiple Grammy and Latin Grammy Award-winning producer. (I'm not kidding.) In an *Inc.* magazine column, I argued that "my biggest strengths—and your biggest strengths—come from *out-side* the chosen field." And for my clients, I recommend that they bring a variety of stimuli into their career for financial and, most importantly, psychological reasons. (We'll get into the financial reasons later in the chapter.)

For those of us in a traditional job setting, then, the job itself sets up the system. Your hours are from 9:30 a.m. to 5:30 p.m., Monday through Friday. Half an hour lunch break. Your office is 15.5 miles away from your home, and your parking spot is in the back left corner of the lot. Are you a morning person, happily getting up before dawn and, to paraphrase the military saying, getting more done before 9 a.m. than most people get done all day? Or are you super-productive on a random weekend day, buoyed by the silent phone notifications and empty email inbox since other people aren't working? So many of us will never know, because we adapted to another person's system instead of discovering our own.

My clients will leave their job, be let go from a long-term commitment, or otherwise be free of a system, and they will be both excited and heartbroken. They are excited because they realize that they hate mornings and feel so much happier—and, as a result, often more creative—burning the midnight oil, or that the need to be productive based on the previous employers' metrics took a psychological toll on them and that they were, and are, way past burnout. They are heartbroken because they were like a fish in water: They were so used to their system that they didn't realize how broken it was. Their system has always been broken. They are just now finding out.

As we'll discuss, there are three layers to building a level of self-sufficiency on your career path: building your own system; creating multiple streams of business; and looking toward a sustainable practice. It doesn't matter if you have a long-standing day job, have a million side hustles, or are an indie businessperson like myself.

First, you have to create an internal system outside of your environment. Again, how can you make sure you are living your best life and contributing at the highest level to those you serve if you aren't sure about your own needs? Your metrics for success need to reflect it. Second, you have to build multiple streams of business. As Sehgal says, there is a nourishment that happens as you create, contribute, and serve in more ways than one. Doing only one job is like marrying someone and expecting them to be your best friend, lover, family member, therapist, and business partner—it puts too much weight on one source and completely skews your ability to be objective about the partnership. Lastly, you have to create toward a sustainable future. One of my favorite questions to ask clients is "Let's go five years into the future. Is what you're doing now sustainable?" If the answer is no, then the system isn't working for you.

In a recent *Akimbo* podcast episode, "Compared to What?," Seth Godin talks about how comparison breeds culture. He uses electricity in the early 1800s as an allegory. And, of course, there was no mainstream electricity in the early 1800s.

> I'm talking about the blackout of 1812. In fact, of all the years before 1812 [and] 1820, 1830, when there was no electricity.

And, no one really missed it. They didn't miss it because their neighbors didn't have electricity. They didn't miss it because they had never had electricity. And so, compared to what? We navigate our days on this planet by looking around, by understanding what is going on in the culture and making a decision about our state.

Our "state" was doing a nine-to-five, raising our income and keeping our debt ratio above it, and assuming that having a socially acceptable job meant security. Until it didn't. For the past year, we've seen some people struggle and, most notably, some people thrive outside of the social norms: working from home, shunning consumerism, and creating their own career path. It's like we've been living without electricity—and suddenly we see our neighbor turn the lights on at night.

The beauty is that the light isn't just with other people. The light is with you too. You just need to turn it on.

And that begins with determining your own system.

CHAPTER 16.

DON'T WORK FOR SYSTEMS, BUT HAVE SYSTEMS WORK FOR YOU

If you are ambitious like myself, then you may have a built-in problem to overcome: We can believe that if things are easy, then they are not worthwhile. We can mistake working hard for things working. We can think mastery is actually failure. I was recently chatting with a colleague, and they asked me my favorite word right now. "Flow," I said. "That's OK!" they responded, "as it's fine to not have to work hard all the time. It's OK to be lazy." I corrected them quickly. Flow isn't the lack of action, definitely not to the point of laziness. (The word "lazy" has its own connotations, from the ironic use toward my hard-working ancestors by the people who enslaved them to the judgment cast upon others for what could be an internal—albeit productive—moment for another person, but let's put that multilayer discussion to the side for now.) Flow is taking account of where you are personally, professionally, emotionally, physically, and where those whom you want to serve are in the same regard, and seeing where you can show up as fully as possible at the moment. It is fluidity. It is not grafting your agenda onto your partnerships, your customers, your life, which can feel as foolish as planting daisies in the dead of winter. It is recognizing the season and acting accordingly.

"It is not the skills we actually have that determine how we feel, but the ones we think we have," Mihaly Csikszentmihalyi says in his book

Flow: The Psychology of Optimum Experience. In other words, you may be great at bookkeeping for yourself—keeping the family budget straight, maximizing discounts, making sure your accounts are never overdrawn— but you may never consider it valuable outside of that particular context because it came to you easily. You don't recognize it as an asset. For example, I can listen to people on end. For as long as I can remember, I could sit and hear and talk with my closest friends and relatives for hours at a time. Communicating, engaging, and—most importantly—unthreading what others say is totally essential to my relationships. Language, both spoken and unspoken, helps me understand those around me, building up my empathy for their unique journey.

Not everyone is like this.

But it took me decades to realize that my deep communication energy—what Seth Godin might call "emotional labor"—was something rare and could be, if I wished, shared beyond my inner circle. It's now why I can coach person after person after person and feel energized rather than depleted, or how I can do an intense keynote, an engaging Q&A, and then go on to connect with folks for the remainder of the day offstage. But I've taken on opportunities where I had a short time onstage with no Q&A— no engagement, based on my needs—or when I had ten minutes to have a deep coaching conversation with a stranger. I managed, but afterward I felt energy-deficient, or incomplete, as if I had left a pile of dirty dishes in the sink as I went out the door.

It didn't match my *flow*. It didn't match my *system*.

In my coaching experience, I've found that flow represents the outer coming-in, and system represents your inner coming-out. Flow is assessing where you want to show up—"showing up" meaning where you want to do your best work, whom you want to serve the most, and how you can be most effective at doing so—and figuring out the best way to make an impact based on the resources you have at the moment. System is the framework you use—"framework" meaning your needs that have to be met, the lens in which you get the nourishment you need to keep showing up, the parts of you that aren't for sale—to keep your foundation intact as the flow ebbs. And it will ebb.

It pairs well with a classic Warren Buffett quote: "Only when the tide goes out do you discover who's been swimming naked." We can push against the flow—the newspaper reporter who refuses to learn any digital skills; the staunch Blockbuster stockholders counting on literally the last video store, in Bend, Oregon, to make a comeback; the saleswoman hustling products that haven't sold in years—but, eventually, it will be clear that we're heading toward burnout, if not worse territory.

So, why don't we upgrade our skills, take a loss on that now-worth-a-penny Blockbuster Video stock, or change what we're selling to fit the times? It's not just ego or sunk cost. It's because it's easier to be reactive than to be proactive. Dan Heath explains in his book *Upstream: How to Solve Problems Before They Happen*, "That's one reason why we tend to favor reaction: because it is more tangible. Downstream work is easier to see, easier to measure. There is a maddening ambiguity about upstream efforts . . . and that requires systems thinking."

In Heath's terminology, "downstream" means fixing stuff after it's already broken, like the doctor putting you on heart medicine, rather than "upstream," perhaps working together with your specialists to create a healthier diet and exercise regimen years before any heart issues occur. Not as exciting, is it? Heath gives an excellent example: A small-town cop was known for issuing a record number of tickets to speeders along the strip. Another cop, though, just parked her vehicle by the main intersection. Just the sight of her car actually caused would-be speeders to slow down, but there was no record that it was working other than a *lower* stack of tickets. If the system rewards police officers based on the number of tickets issued, then the cop doing the systemic, upstream thinking would actually be rewarded less than the one who was making the reactionary, downstream decisions.

The coronavirus pandemic is an excellent example of flow versus system. For many of us, our inner system was strictly based on outer circumstances of flow: the daily commute framed our day, not our kissing our partner in the morning or tucking our kids or older relatives in at night; our time spent in our neighborhood squeezed between work, errands, and perhaps long-distance travel, not our prioritizing saying "Hello" to those literally next door; our career goals tied to the proverbial "how many tickets served," not based on the impact we have on others. To be clear, there is absolutely nothing wrong with these metrics reflecting your values, as there are loving lifelong bachelors and bachelorettes who live for work, consider their neighborhood a launch pad rather than a sanctuary, and regard their title and bank account the ultimate scoreboard of their life. Hell, until I met my partner years ago, I designed my entire life—as an independent, freelance-writing apartment renter—so I could move to another city, if not even another country, at a moment's notice. I don't regret for a moment living in, at rough count, more than two dozen places from Chicago to New Orleans to San Francisco. But those metrics reflected my values—*until they didn't*. Then those metrics changed, and I'm happily settled in Las Vegas, helping lead my family and eagerly getting on the road with them post-pandemic. The separation—the cognitive dissonance, as coaches like to say—is in that many of us didn't realize that our system didn't reflect our values. It is because our metrics for success were likely given to us by an outside entity, like the culture we were raised in, the expectations of our first job many, many years ago, or our monetary needs of the moment, even if that moment had passed a while back.

But we often don't slow down enough to realize that our values have changed. It often takes a sudden shock—like, well, a global pandemic—for us to pump the brakes and realize that where we are at and, more concerning, where we are headed isn't where we intended at all. Following flow isn't laziness; but doing so without having a framework in place means you are just reacting to circumstances. As I often say to my clients, how can you make your singular impact on the world if you are only reacting to the world?

"We have an unprecedented opportunity right now to reinvent, to create workplace culture almost from scratch," Joanne Lipman writes in *Time* magazine. "Over the past decades, various types of businesses have rotated in and out of favor—conglomerates in the '60s, junk bonds in the '80s, tech in the '00s—but the basic workplace structure, of office cubicles and face time, has remained the same." The opportunity, she argues, is for our work to be better built around our lives, not the other way around. As she notes, in March 2020, as most of the Western world went into shelter in place, statistics show job turnover at an all-time low with Americans "just hoping to hang on to what they had, even if they hated their jobs." A year later, as we emerged with vaccine rollouts and other scientific knowledge, experts warned that The Great Resignation was coming.

Wait, so you said we absolutely had to be in the office to do our job, but we suddenly had the option to work from home when faced with an apocalypse, and now you're telling us to come back in the building? We feared for our lives—perhaps we still do—and now I am expected to spend most of my day fulfilling some obscure metric? Isn't what I'm doing with my life supposed to matter? Wasn't that implied, if not directly said to me, during the job interview process? How the hell did I get here?

These conversations happen all the time. They are not new to the pandemic or even to this generation. I've heard them and helped parse them many times over the years. They are usually whispers, individual crises or struggles, within what Pink Floyd might call hanging on in quiet desperation. With the pandemic, those whispers turned into a primal scream.

"As the postpandemic great reopening unfolds, millions of others are also reassessing their relationship to their jobs," Lipman says. "The modern office was created after World War II, on a military model—strict hierarchies, created by men for men, with an assumption that there is a wife to handle duties at home. But after years of gradual change in Silicon Valley and elsewhere, there's a growing realization that the model is broken. Millions of people have spent the past year reevaluating their priorities. How much time do they want to spend in an office? Where do they want to live if they can work remotely? Do they want to switch careers? For many, this has become a moment to literally redefine what *is* work."

I love this breakdown, as it reveals two ways we can confuse our career with our work. First, we cheat ourselves when we believe systems cannot change. As Lipman notes, today's office system was established back in the 1940s. At the time, television was black-and-white where it existed at all, computers were the size of large rooms, and my grandmother, who recently passed at 88, was the age of my third-grade son. Why doesn't the system still work? Perhaps we didn't check under the hood. Perhaps we didn't *want* to check under the hood. "Every system is perfectly designed to get the results it gets," Heath says beautifully in *Upstream.* "Good intentions cannot overcome bad systems." To flip back on what was just said, the system is working fine. It's been working fine. It's just the desired results—or, to put on a more proletarian lens, our willingness and tolerance to sacrifice for those results has lessened. Whether macro or micro, at the world at large or how you structure your personal life, what you have when you don't recognize the system is a setup reflective of the very last time you thought about it—or, in the case of the modern workplace, a nearly century-old setup. I'm the primary caregiver of our eight- and five-year-old boys, while my wife is a pediatrician seeing patients. As hosts Doug French and Jeff Bogle and I shared on a recent Dad 2.0 podcast episode, our dads in the sixties and seventies would have had a ridiculously hard climb to create the same dynamic I have with my spouse. And my aforementioned grandmother's mother and father, both of whom would have been in the workplace in the 1940s? Some workplaces required the husband's or father's permission for a woman to work there, and let's not even get into things like birth control and an independent bank account. No wonder the framework doesn't fit. But to further Heath and Lipman's points, the main goal of the 1940s workplace was to create an efficient, post-war workforce. The system is designed for that. Not work–life balance, work–life integration, or work–life whatever. It was designed to extract as much value as possible from each worker, the Henry Ford assembly-line dream applied to white-collar work and beyond. Good intentions like paternity leave, unlimited vacation, and ping-pong tables—popular in my time in circa 2008 Silicon Valley—cannot overcome bad systems. And the pandemic broke the system. The companies know it. The employees know it. We all know it. And we can't go back.

Hence, The Great Resignation.

"We aren't supposed to live to work," one recent resignator told *Time* magazine. "We're supposed to work to live."

Second, on Lipman's discussion on career and work, career is the way we are currently making an impact. Our work—or Work with a capital "W," as Oprah Winfrey has said—is the impact we are committed to making. In my instance, my career résumé says I am a one-on-one business coach, the author of more than two dozen books, and a TED Speaker four times over. My Work is helping side hustlers, solopreneurs, and other non-traditional entrepreneurs—as well as those in the BIPOC, LGBTQ, or other communities that are overlooked and underfunded—to find their own power in their voice. It doesn't matter if my career is as an *Inc.* magazine columnist, as a public speaker, or as a YouTube show host. The message is more important than the medium. Your career is the flow. Your Work is the system. You bring your system with you wherever you go, no matter what the circumstances.

As I mentioned previously, I launched my #BringYourWorth show in late 2020. It was, in part, a response from a public speaker who couldn't go out in public! My career, as in my persona as well as how I got paid, was in going on a stage and talking to and with people for 45 minutes at a time. My Work, as in my personal system, was to show up as much as possible for the aforementioned non-traditional entrepreneur. It wasn't tied to things flowing a certain way. And because it wasn't tied to my having to be onstage, then my business actually grew during our pandemic year. For you personally, the system, the purpose, the Work continues, regardless of the situations you are put in by outside circumstances.

Strong personal systems perform, regardless of flow.

And, like a strong current, you can pick up treasures along the way from any circumstances. The more grounded you are, the more you recognize them.

I shared as much in *Bring Your Worth*, my 2017 book that feels more relevant in a post-pandemic world:

> The circumstances delivering you pain will eventually recede, through time or through tolerance or through insight, but the wisdom gained will remain, glistening on the shore like seashells. The pain will go away. Do not be angry at the circumstances, or at the situations, or at the luck. You cannot be angry at a particular moment in your life without being ungrateful for the riches it gave you. One cannot exist without the other. They are one and the same.

The Greek and Chinese words for chaos are virtually synonymous with another term: opportunity. We can make the most progress when things are uprooted and previous boundaries blur. It just doesn't feel like it. Our perceived loss requires us to reach higher than before. We now have no past to defend.

Corporations have sold their massive office spaces to stop hemorrhaging overhead money. Powerful leaders and brave employees alike are recognizing how out-of-whack their personal lives have been. And technology is affording us more options and freedom than at any other time in human history.

The ground is soft now, which means systems both large and personal can be changed permanently.

Think about how you would live your best life doing your Work. And realize that the once-in-a-century window for creating systemic change personally and professionally is closing as we speak.

→

CHAPTER 17.

UNDERSTAND PASSIVE INCOME AND OTHER OPPORTUNITIES AVAILABLE TO ALL

O ne of the worst feelings in the world is to quit your job, go independent, or put your all into a new business idea—and realize that your bank account is dropping like a hot potato. I experienced this when I took on a well-paying temp job to help make ends meet. I had just gotten my grad degree and was getting my feet wet as a freelance writer—that is, making a full-time living as a journalist for different publications. Like most indie vocations, your network is your net worth, and I didn't have much of a network yet. No one knew who I was, so no one was willing to give me a contract blind. I needed time to build trust with the editors with whom I wanted to work. This promise of future work didn't quite resonate with my Chicago landlord. So, I took a temp job during the day and wrote my ass off at night. Soon, I was writing for *Playboy* as well as more humble publications. The writing alone wasn't enough to make ends meet, but soon I got a peachy opportunity to write a ton of articles for a new publication. In fact, it would be enough to cover my rent, by far my biggest expense, for at least two months.

I gave notice after I signed the contract.

The day job was more than supportive. They even had a going-away lunch break with punch and cookies! They were more than kind.

I went home on the El beaming. "Finally," I thought to myself, "I can be a *real* writer!"

The next morning, my friend who had connected me to the gig said I needed to call them right away.

"They just declared bankruptcy," they said. My gig was worth about four thousand dollars. I knew my friend's role was worth in the tens of thousands.

"What happens now?" I ask.

"Well, they have a court hearing next week."

And just as suddenly, I didn't know how I was going to pay my rent. Again.

I did go to the court hearings (there were more than one) and got my money in pennies on the dollar. Maybe a couple hundred dollars over the course of the following two years? In the end, my planned "steady income" became a bittersweet surprise in the mail every six months or so.

It is a lesson we all learn: IOUs aren't income. Contracts can be reneged. Customer commitments don't count until the transaction is made. Some of us are luckier than others. I learned it in the first year of my long independent career. I just suffered a few ramen-fueled weeks, not losing a house, starving my family, or getting the car repo'd.

What lesson we learn, though, is drastically different. We sometimes believe we aren't talented or good enough to hack it. The comparison game is strong today, especially considering that my career began when Mark Zuckerberg was still in high school and Twitter was something only bird-watchers said. We can also think any type of independent hustle is meant for so-called "trust-fund babies" and the wealthy. This, of course, is often not true: like many colleagues, I made a full-time living as an independent for a decade and a half before my wife and I married, and even now we carry our respective weight with our resources. I was on the board of the American Society of Journalists and Authors, and I know the stats—many of us freelance writers make a modest living and choose to live a minimalist or thoughtful lifestyle to support it. (It is also why, like in other indie professions, adding regular increases to your rates—as little as 10 percent per year—can change your entire career financial picture.)

What I learned was that I couldn't be dependent on outside entities for my well-being. I learned that I needed to have some financial structure, some framework, that had absolutely nothing to do with the capricious whims of publications, invoices lost in the black hole of accounting or, in the time of snailmail, the competence of the mail service.

What I discovered was passive income.

I was pitching a tech-trend feature article to a major publication, but they weren't interested. It was then that I thought, "This feels like a big idea. Maybe I should write a book? And if I write the book, *then* they'll see the big idea and *then* I can write a bunch more articles for them!" Keep in mind that I had no intention of becoming an author. I was a freelance journalist. That was my identity. So any action I took should get me closer to being more of a freelance journalist. (Not to mention my minimizing the book process. The book idea, *Porn & Pong: How Grand Theft Auto, Tomb Raider and Other Sexy Games Changed Our Culture*, would take five years to publish. I wasn't even thirty at the time.)

Then it hit me: "Wait: I can do a 15,000-word feature article at a dollar a word for a major publication—good money—and get $15,000 once. Or I can research a little bit more, do a 40,000-word book manuscript, and then I will get paid every single time someone buys the book *forever*?"

I was sitting in my attic apartment, alone, talking to myself.

"Why the fuck didn't anyone tell me?!"

I had just graduated from the number-one journalism school in the country. I had three strong, capable parents—my dad, my mom, and my step-dad. I had built a network of wonderful mentors. But no one knew. In journalism school, as my writing colleague Jeanette Hurt and I say in our book *The Passive Writer*, we're taught to deep-dive into a story, get paid for that one story by salary or per-word rate, and then move on to the next story. My parents understood real estate, and all three by now have spent most of their careers as independents, but it still ended up being what *Earn Your Leisure* co-founder Rashad Bilal calls "trading time for money." And my mentors at the time, however visionary, did not share anything beyond raising your rate and hustling smarter.

No one told me, which is why I'm telling you.

Passive income is creating something once, and then getting paid multiple times for it. You get paid as long as the people you serve are interested in what you created. That can mean forever.

In your career remix, passive income matters because it allows you security as you develop your next act. Too often, we don't monitor how we feel or how toxic our environment might be; and when we do recognize it, we make a hasty decision to leave our job, quit our career, or otherwise run away and join the circus. (Not that there's anything wrong with the circus. I know professional clowns, and it is a serious profession. *We* just don't take it seriously, hence the euphemism.) We recognize our discontent, take action, and then figure out how we will fund whatever transition we're in. That's backward. It *is* a transition, and all transitions take time. And while a part-time job, as I had had after grad school, may help you navigate the gap, it still requires taking time away from your new work to do your older or lesser work.

The best passive incomes also help level your financial picture so you can do things like, well, budget effectively. The more independent a career you pursue, the less predictable your income will be. If you are accustomed to a fixed direct deposit every other Friday—and get heart palpitations when it happens to be delayed a day because of a bank holiday you forgot about—then the space between traditional jobs or the completely freelance space will be quite a shock. Particularly early in my career, it wasn't unusual for me to get paid a solid five figures for a lucrative gig, and then not get another paycheck for months. Suddenly, that five or even six-figure opportunity starts to look mighty thin once you have to stretch it over twelve or eighteen months, not taking into account your taxes (higher for the self-employed), health insurance, and retirement fund. To paraphrase one freelancer, my bank account either is $17,589.51 or it is $.39. Mike Michalowicz's classic *Profit First: Transform Your Business from a Cash-Eating Monster to a Money-Making Machine* is required reading for managing your independent income, whether it is from a full-time hustle or a side hustle accompanying your day job. In short, you have to pay yourself in steady increments—essentially give yourself a salary—based on the lump sums you receive. It helps you flatten the ups and downs so you don't spend too much during the fat times and get too close to broke during the lean times. Unfortunately, even the best techniques won't help you if you don't have income coming in. Steady passive income streams mean you are receiving money, whether your main money is high or low.

My business currently has four passive income categories: books, journalism, classes, and shows. As shown in my earlier revelation, books are the clearest passive income for me: spend months to years writing something, and then people can theoretically buy it forever, which means I will be paid forever and, because I own the rights to my work, my descendants will be paid well after I'm gone too. All my business books are available in paperback, digital, audiobook, and, in some cases, hardcover, and each version provides its own passive income stream. Journalism passive income is through my column for *Inc.* magazine, at www.incdamonbrown.com. We essentially have a profit-sharing commitment: when someone visits the website and reads a column, *Inc.* magazine gets money through advertising. It takes a cut and I take a cut. The beauty is that I've done more than five hundred columns, so it isn't unusual for me to get a three-figure or even four-figure check from a column I wrote years ago that just happened to gain popularity again. Classes include my side-hustle boot camp currently through the online platform Teachable at paylancing.teachable.com. First launched in parallel to my best seller *The Bite-Sized Entrepreneur*, the boot camp is an intensive, self-directed class based around the principles in the book. I spent weeks recording videos and designing the course, and, about once a year, I update the material with my latest book. Otherwise, it is an experience I can offer to people who want something deeper than my books—and they get something similar to a coaching experience, but I don't actually have to coach them directly. Lastly, the show passive income is from my #BringYourWorth YouTube program. Started in late 2020, I currently do a fifteen-minute show every Monday, Wednesday, and Friday discussing a specific skill from my coaching practice like goal setting, time management, and, without irony, passive income. As the show grows, YouTube will begin to add appropriate advertisements during the program. Not unlike *Inc.* magazine, YouTube and I will split the cut from the advertisers. I record one fifteen-minute video; it has the potential for infinite income.

All these examples represent what business strategists call a shift from the one-to-one to the one-to-many. If you are a plumber, then you can only do so much business: you are the one with the knowledge and you are the one with the tools. You physically cannot cater to more than one household, office, or building. If you teach others how to fix their toilets, then you may initially make less per customer, but you can bring on exponentially more customers and may be able to bring in those customers by doing only one job (like writing a book or doing a video).

You may have caught the reason why most of us do not create passive income: we have to do the work up front, often for little to no pay.

My *Inc.* magazine column paid very little until I built up an audience. My #BringYourWorth channel is still going toward monetization. The rub is that if you invest in the work now, then passive income becomes a "set it and forget it" model later. I regularly get checks from books I wrote more than a decade ago and, once my #BringYourWorth show does monetize, then I'll have hundreds of episodes that my audience can enjoy like a Netflix binge. (It is also creating a great proof-of-concept as a public speaker, coach, or author, as potential customers see that I know my subject matter well.)

As Jeanette Hurt and I share in *The Passive Writer*, developing my passive income streams wasn't just a nicety. They actually helped me keep food on the table during one of my slower periods, particularly with the launch of my first online boot camp:

> Designing this course took only a few hours a week since he already had written four books on the topic, but the impact on his income was tremendous. His "active" income checks finally started arriving in mid-to-late February, but his passive income checks kept his business humming along quite nicely. For the first six weeks of 2018, Damon lived on only the residuals from all of the work he accomplished weeks, months, and even as much as a dozen years before. Without consciously creating passive income, Damon would have had zero new cash at the start of 2018.

My experience can apply to your going independent after having a traditional job, as well as to your being in between traditional jobs. In fact, it may be even more relevant when you're looking for another job, as we tend to think the next job opportunity will come faster than it will. Worse, because we look at our unemployment as a temporary state, we may not dedicate as much time as we should to creating a serious income system.

When it comes to funding your next phase, *Pivot* author and business coach Jenny Blake talks about three important factors: burn rate, runway, and bridge income. The first two are common startup terms. Burn rate means how quickly you will spend the money you've got, and runway means how long that money will last. For instance, if my monthly household needs add up to $2,000 and I have $10,000 available, then my burn rate is $2,000/month and my runway is five months. Think about your bringing in new money as your plane is taking off: you need to get it going before you run out of runway!

Bridge income is an even more interesting concept. Traditionally, a bridge loan is short-term financing used to hold things over while you implement the plan for long-term financing, Blake writes; and "bridge income tides you over while making a change, but is not your desired primary long-term solution."

Bridge income could be a part-time job you take to help ends meet, adding a few extra shifts to your current day job, or creating an active side hustle alongside your main work. These options may last a while, but Blake emphasizes that bridge income is meant to facilitate your making it through the gap between where you are now and where you want to be later. It's also worth noting that your nest egg, rainy-day fund, or otherwise stashed cash is not bridge income. Income, by definition, means it comes from an outside source.

"Although your savings can act as bridge income, this is not ideal for two reasons: savings are a finite source, and the more you spend, the more you may stress out, impairing your ability to think creatively. Treat your savings as a backup account that you only dip into if your bridge income fails," Blake writes in *Pivot*.

This is where passive income gets really powerful. The money isn't like a fixed savings account that will, at best, stay the same (and, with the paltry American interest rates as of this writing, you'll even be losing your financial power because of inflation). Instead, it is a flow of money that requires little or no management on your part, freeing you to focus on creating your next act.

To figure out your best passive income opportunities, lean into three basic tenets: do something once and get paid multiple times; use what you've already got; and determine what people are always asking you for.

First, it's worth repeating that passive income is meant to be created once and, at most, modified and updated later. Crocheting blankets isn't passive income, no matter how fast you are—unless you're renting the blankets to people and charging them each time they pass them around! The dual purpose of passive income is to give you revenue as you proverbially sleep; and, because of that revenue, to free up your energy so you can focus on the bigger picture of your business.

Second, the best passive income opportunities often come from what we already know. For my #BringYourWorth show, I studied my favorite YouTube hosts, thought about the best format, and learned the technical ins and outs of lighting, editing, and so forth. What I didn't have to work on, though, were my subject matter, my schedule commitment, or my public speaking. When the show launched, I had already written six business books focused on side hustlers, solopreneurs, and other non-traditional entrepreneurs. I knew my audience and how to serve them best. I had already done more than five hundred *Inc.* magazine columns and hundreds of other scheduled columns for publications over the years. I was used to committing to a programming routine—in this case, every Monday, Wednesday, and Friday at 11:30 a.m., Pacific—and sticking to it through the long haul. Lastly, I had already spent several years as a paid public speaker and completed my fourth TED Talk earlier that same year. I knew how to speak clearly, keep salient points, and engage with the audience—and, luckily, had gotten lots of virtual speaking experience earlier that year. Let's be clear: the thought of starting a YouTube show made me nervous as hell! But in retrospect, this type of business move matched my skill set well. In my coaching, I see passive income pursuits fail most often when someone is trying too hard to come up with an idea that doesn't fit their strengths—or, worse, doesn't fit what they even care about. You won't see me launching a YouTube channel dedicated to mayonnaise or to bland food, because I hate them both. Use the same measurement yourself. Remember, you'll often be putting the work in before you even see a dime. You should actually like it.

Finally, the strongest passive income opportunities are based on things people are already asking you for. To paraphrase author Dorie Clark, where are you a known expert? Don't mistake this for being a celebrity, as few of us are. Rather, what are people always asking you about? As I mentioned earlier, people recognize me as a patient listener, so they are more likely to share detailed, honest stories. I don't think it is a coincidence that I became a journalist as a teenager and, much later, became a business coach. Those special traits that are recognized by others—Jeanette Hurt and I call them your "superpowers"—give hints at where your best passive income opportunities lie.

It's worth noting that these aren't powers you grant yourself: we can have an awful time actually seeing our biggest strengths while simultaneously we overvalue ourselves where we are average, if not deficient. For instance, multiple studies have found that the average American considers themselves an "above-average driver." Statistically, of course, the individual assessment can't possibly be accurate, as the mathematics of the average means that most of the individuals asked would fall in the middle. Anecdotally, have you seen how people drive? Calling their self-awareness laughable would be more than kind. Our poor view of self falls into what's called the Johari window. Created by psychologists Harrington Ingham and Joseph Luft, the Johari window—a combination of their first names—is set up like a window pane with four quadrants:

The upper-left-hand quadrant: Things you know about yourself and other people know about you. This is what you're known for.

The upper-right-hand quadrant: Things other people know about you, but you don't know about yourself. This is what you aren't aware of.

The lower-left-hand quadrant: Things you know about yourself, but others don't know about you. This is what you keep secret or private.

The lower-right-hand quadrant: Things neither you nor other people know about you. This is what no one knows.

So you may *think* you're good at explaining your field of, say, accounting, but may not realize that other people aren't understanding you as much as you think. It's a key reason to build your network, as we talked about in part V of this book, Build Alliances as You Create Your Best Business Brand. This is always relevant, but it's doubly so before you start pursuing a passive income opportunity—you don't want to build your next venture based on a skill set you don't actually have.

A great rule of thumb is that you can never call yourself a "thought leader," "visionary," or the culturally offensive term "guru." By definition, other people have to call you that.

Passive income should not be considered a bonus, a luxury, or nice to have. Pursuing it should not even be tied to your being dissatisfied with your job, being between jobs, or building an independent hustle. It should always be on your radar. Indie musicians get the lion's share of their money from touring, but what happens when you suddenly can't tour? "Our income went to zero," one musician told NBC News in September 2020, six months into America's shelter in place, with another adding "It didn't matter if you were U2 or the songwriter next door, the plug had been pulled. No touring." The relationship with a supervisor could be stellar, but what if they are let go and the perks, benefits, and even commitments you agreed to weren't in the actual contract? Relationships are the fabric of power. There is no guarantee that the person you have a relationship with will keep *their* power, though, which means your station in the work culture is never guaranteed.

You always need to have power sources outside of your day job, independent of the fickle economy, and beyond the ups and downs of your personal life. Establishing passive income creates the foundation to keep you afloat not only financially but psychologically too.

→

CHAPTER 18.

BUILD A SUSTAINABLE
APPROACH TO YOUR CAREER

What is the best outcome for you? For all of us? It is you, creating your own culture. The problem is that we rely on other people, organizations, or, worse, faceless crowds to tell us our value—perhaps confirmed in giving us money, perhaps implied by crowning us with empty titles—and therefore we look to them for guidance on the best way to serve. Our inner voice begins to go quiet. In fact, we believe that the enablers are our inner voice. That works for a bit, maybe even for a while, but eventually you will be unplugged. The job will be eliminated. The favorite supervisor will be moved. The company will merge. The role initially given will change. The opinion of the majority will change. And all the energy, all that confidence and assuredness, all that faithfulness was poured into a foundation that wasn't even yours. Jay-Z has a wonderful line that says, paraphrasing, don't fight over turf that your family's renting. We turn our jobs into our lifeline—our real social network, our spouse we spend the most time with, our determiner of values—and fall apart when the circumstances change. But we were pouring into someone else's dream and forgot it wasn't ours.

You don't have to become the founder of a company. But you do have to become the founder of your own career. A job shouldn't be giving you an opportunity to shine. You should lean into how you want to shine within the job. My clients who have succeeded the most aren't looking for a position, title, or gig to tell them who they are. They have done the work and are so clear on what they are—and what they are not—that they see each potential position, title, or gig as a way to make an impact most aligned with their mission and values. That is culture, and they bring their personal culture wherever they go.

"Culture says, 'These are our standards. These are the things that are sacrosanct. And in any spaces that aren't carved out, you can do anything you want, because that enables the market economy that enriches so many of us,'" Seth Godin said on his podcast, *Akimbo*. "And that is part of the challenge we're facing in our culture today: It is tempting to say 'I am responsible for everything that I do—leave me alone!' But the rivers, the rivers of time, the rivers of connection, the rivers of culture, and the rivers of rivers are now far more intertwined than they have ever been before. So when we put an idea in a kid's head, it will pay dividends for generations to come."

The river analogy—from Godin here, from Dan Heath's *Upstream* mentioned earlier, from my own coaching practice—is apt for career journeys. Even the most rapid waters don't change quickly. They pick things up, they let things go, they refresh, and they reset. They evolve slowly, over time, just as their biggest impacts on their environments, like the Grand Canyon, come from steady, persistent, deliberate action.

Investors have a fabulous term: dollar-cost averaging. It sounds dry, but it is magical. You commit to putting a certain fixed amount into a financial investment regularly. The only two things you need to decide are what you can comfortably always afford and with what frequency you'd like to invest. For instance, it could be $50 every two weeks. And you do that as long as you see fit. That's it. The beauty is that you invest no matter what the market is doing. The market is up? You invest $50. The market is down? You invest $50. The investment is trending on social media? You invest $50. Financial-news shows are shitting on your investment decision? You invest

$50. All of this doesn't matter. None of it matters. Because you've already made a commitment based on your own values. You made the commitment before you even started.

Dollar-cost averaging means you've committed to showing up, no matter what.

What if we overlaid that same principle over how much quality and effort we regularly put into our careers? How much we dedicated to learning more about our craft? How we treated others? Or how we treated ourselves? What potential Grand Canyon–size dividends would eventually come out of that?

And studies found that in most markets, the dollar-cost-averaging investors end up having more long-term upside than investors trying to predict the highs and buy at the lows. Their predictions are usually wrong. They would have been better off just steadily investing.

"We have to understand the interplay between intensity and consistency. You can't go to the gym for nine hours and get into shape. It doesn't work," Simon Sinek says. "But if you work out every day for twenty minutes, you will absolutely get into shape. The problem is, I don't know when."

And if you're steadily investing in yourself, you don't need to know when.

Isn't it time to hit the gym?

TAKE THE BUILD FROM NOW QUIZ

Curious about your biggest resource at the moment? Take this quick quiz.

Answer each question as instinctively as possible. Match the answers and see your strongest resource.

For a deeper discovery, go to www.buildfromnowquiz.com.

1. **I worry most about:**
   a. Finishing what I start
   b. Missing opportunities because I'm busy
   c. Losing interest in what I begin
   d. Obsessing over what I'm into at the moment

2. **My friends would say I:**
   a. Always follow through
   b. Make the most out of uncomfortable situations
   c. Do things in the most efficient manner
   d. Always go the extra mile when it comes to quality

3. **I feel most alive when I:**
   a. Work from a blank slate
   b. Push myself harder than I ever have before
   c. Know I have room to learn and correct my mistakes
   d. Deep-dive into one concept or idea

If I said:

1a & 2a

1a & 3d or

2a & 3d

Then my biggest resource is **FOCUS**

If I said:

1b & 2b

1b & 3a or

2b & 3a

Then my biggest resource is **AGILITY**

If I said:

1c & 2c

1c & 3c or

2c & 3c

Then my biggest resource is **TIME**

If I said:

1d & 2d

1d & 3b or

2d & 3b

Then my biggest resource is **ENERGY**

If I said none of these matches, then my biggest resources are Balanced at the moment.

CONNECT WITH DAMON

This book is just the beginning of your growth. Here's how we keep the conversation going.

Get Bonus Content and More

http://www.JoinDamon.me

Get your free business toolkit to gain even more insight into your next steps. You'll also get exclusive content, early previews of new goodies, and a weekly discussion with fellow creators!

Watch #BringYourWorth show

http://www.youtube.com/browndamon

Catch Damon's free #BringYourWorth show every Monday, Wednesday, and Friday at 11:30 AM, PT, to get coaching insights, passive income strategies, and even live Q&As. Subscribe for free and don't miss an episode.

One-on-One Guidance

http://www.damonbrown.net

I've worked with hundreds of clients and connected with thousands of creatives. I'd love to help you organize your priorities, apply the Build From Now method, and make room for your best career. We can set up a time to chat and see if we're a good fit. Reach out at damon@damonbrown.net.

Do the Bite-Sized Entrepreneur Boot Camp

http://paylancing.teachable.com

This six-part self-guided course will bring the best out of your current productivity, focus, and creativity. Taking the book series a step farther, The Bite-Sized Entrepreneur boot camp is perfect to do at your own pace with my guidance through video, audio, and text. Join through JoinDamon.me to get a special discount on one-on-one coaching opportunities!

Speaking at Your Event

http://www.damonbrown.net

I am happy to talk about your event and how a discussion on mindfulness, productivity, or entrepreneurship can best fit your needs. International venues are welcome, as are US events, and my platforms include TED, Colombia 4.0 in Bogota, and American University in Washington, DC. My keynote talks are also available and discussed in detail in the next section, Available Keynote Talks.

Available Keynote Talks

http://www.damonbrown.net

Damon is available to speak virtually, offsite, and in person worldwide at select events, conferences, and companies. His audiences have included the main TED Conference, second stage, in British Columbia; American Underground tech incubator in Durham, NC; Colombia 4.0 in Bogota, Colombia; the Adult Entertainment Expo in Las Vegas; and American University in Washington, DC. He has worked with Google, Salesforce, and many other corporations. Damon's talks interweave personal narrative and industry knowledge with actionable strategies. He is also happy to include Q&As and panel discussions as well as moderating panels and interviewing other leaders.

Reach out at damon@damonbrown.net.

Profit

How to Create Your True Worth

Creatives often undervalue their services to the market, to their bank account, and to the world. In this inspirational and practical talk, Damon shares the best ways we can joyfully make a living from our craft, create business partnerships worthy of our skills, and truly be of service to others.

Productivity

The Power of Good Enough

What is the number-one killer of innovation? Perfection. With perfection, the key motivation often isn't having high standards, but being afraid of making a mistake. In this talk, I share the three powerful strengths you get when you let perfection go.

Entrepreneurship

Why Your Side Hustle Matters More than Ever

Believe it or not, we already have most of the skills we need to create our passion-driven business. So why aren't most people pursuing their potentially profitable ideas? They are intimidated by the small gap in their skill set. In this immediately actionable talk, Damon shares how to easily traverse that gap and explains the three crucial strengths every successful entrepreneur possesses. It is an inspiring talk for both potential entrepreneurs and ambitious upstarts.

SIGNIFICANT REFERENCES

Opening Quote

Sun Tzu quote. Sun Tzu. *The Art of War (Audiobook performed by Aidan Gillen)* (Audible / Public Domain, 2005).

The Noble Pig

Dweck, Carol. *Mindset: The New Psychology of Success* (Ballantine Books, 2007).

Sims, Peter. *Little Bets: How Breakthrough Ideas Emerge from Small Discoveries* (Simon & Schuster, 2011).

Brown, Damon. *The Ultimate Bite-Sized Entrepreneur Trilogy: 76 Ways to Boost Time, Productivity & Focus on Your Big Idea* (Bring Your Worth, 2017).

I. Establish Your Own New Normal: Intro

Brené Brown quote. Brown, Brené. *Rising Strong: How the Ability to Reset Transforms the Way We Live, Love, Parent, and Lead* (Random House, 2017).

Clinehens, Jennifer. *Choice Hacking* (A Medium Publication), "The Halo Effect: How to Use Psychology to Perfect Your Experience." Originally published June 2020. Currently available online: https://medium.com/choice-hacking/the-halo-effect-how-to-use-psychology-to-perfect-your-experience-d8362e921653

"Carnegie Mellon Research Explores Nostalgic Preferences: Why the Past Seems Better." Originally published June 2013. Currently available online: https://www.cmu.edu/news/stories/archives/2013/june/june26_nostalgicpreferences.html

Brown, Brené. *Rising Strong: How the Ability to Reset Transforms the Way We Live, Love, Parent, and Lead* (Random House, 2017).

Brown, Damon. *Bring Your Worth: How to Level Up Your Creative Power, Value & Service to the World* (Bring Your Worth, 2017).

Make Your Own Metrics for Success

Hendricks, Gay. *The Big Leap: Conquer Your Hidden Fear and Take Life to the Next Level* (HarperOne, 2009).

Csikszentmihalyi, Mihaly. *Flow: The Psychology of Optimal Experience* (Harper Perennial Modern Classics, 2008).

Wiest, Brianna. *Forbes*, "How to Get Into the Zone of Genius and Unlock Your Highest Potential." Originally published September 2018. Currently available online: https://www.forbes.com/sites/briannawiest/2018/09/26/how-to-get-into-the-zone-of-genius-and-unlock-your-highest-potential/?sh=6327e4fc5672

Godin, Seth. *The Icarus Deception: How High Will You Fly?* (Portfolio, 2012).

Brown, Damon. *Inc.*, "Regain Emotional Control with This Powerful, Explicit Quote." Originally published February 2018. Currently available online: https://www.inc.com/damon-brown/this-powerful-explicit-quote-will-help-you-quickly-regain-emotional-intelligence.html

Brown, Damon. *Build From Now: How to Know Your Power, See Your Abundance & Nourish the World* (Bring Your Worth, 2021).

Brown, Damon. *The Ultimate Bite-Sized Entrepreneur Trilogy: 76 Ways to Boost Time, Productivity & Focus on Your Big Idea* (Bring Your Worth, 2017).

Dweck, Carol. *Mindset: The New Psychology of Success* (Ballantine Books, 2007).

Johnson, Whitney. *Disrupt Yourself, with a New Introduction: Master Relentless Change and Speed Up Your Learning Curve* (Harvard Business Review Press, 2019).

Duhigg, Charles. *The Power of Habit: Why We Do What We Do in Life and Business* (Random House, 2014).

Guillebeau, Chris. *Side Hustle: From Idea to Income in 27 Days* (Currency, 2017).

Godin, Seth. *The Practice: Shipping Creative Work* (Portfolio, 2020).

Design Your Life Around Your Career, Not Vice Versa
Brown, Damon. *Inc.*, "How to Make More Space for Your Dreams." Originally published January 2020. Currently available online: https://www.inc.com/damon-brown/how-to-make-more-space-for-your-dreams.html

Mac, Ryan. *Forbes*, "Inside the Post-Minecraft Life of Billionaire Gamer God Markus Persson." Originally published March 2015. Currently available online: https://www.forbes.com/sites/ryanmac/2015/03/03/minecraft-markus-persson-life-after-microsoft-sale/?sh=6e9f78d61616

Jarvis, Paul. *Company of One: Why Staying Small Is the Next Big Thing for Business* (Mariner Books, 2019).

Brown, Damon, and Jeanette Hurt. *The Passive Writer: 5 Ways to Earn Money in Your Sleep* (Bring Your Worth, 2018).

Brown, Damon. *The Ultimate Bite-Sized Entrepreneur Trilogy: 76 Ways to Boost Time, Productivity & Focus on Your Big Idea* (Bring Your Worth, 2017).

Brown, Damon. *Inc.*, "Feel Like a Failure at Your Day Job? It May Mean Success." Originally published September 2019. Currently available online: https://www.inc.com/damon-brown/feeling-like-a-failure-with-a-day-job-it-may-mean-success.html

Brown, Damon. *Build From Now: How to Know Your Power, See Your Abundance & Nourish the World* (Bring Your Worth, 2021).

Set Your Life Goals

Brown, Damon. *Inc.*, "Feel Like a Failure at Your Day Job? It May Mean Success." Originally published September 2019. Currently available online: https://www.inc.com/damon-brown/feeling-like-a-failure-with-a-day-job-it-may-mean-success.html

Brown, Brené. *Rising Strong: How the Ability to Reset Transforms the Way We Live, Love, Parent, and Lead* (Random House, 2017).

Sins, Peter. *Little Bets: How Breakthrough Ideas Emerge from Small Discoveries* (Simon & Schuster, 2011).

Brown, Damon. *Inc.*, "Why Difficult Limitations Make You a Better Entrepreneur." Originally published May 2016. Currently available online: https://www.inc.com/damon-brown/why-your-limitations-make-you-a-better-entrepreneur.html

Curtin, Melanie. *Inc.*, "Oprah's Brilliant Career Advice for 20-Somethings Is a Master Class in Emotional Intelligence." Originally published October 2017. Currently available online: https://www.inc.com/melanie-curtin/oprah-says-this-is-1-question-all-millennials-should-ask-themselves-regarding-their-career.html

Carter, Christine. *The Sweet Spot: How to Accomplish More by Doing Less* (Ballantine Books, 2017).

Brown, Damon. *Inc.*, "Why Entrepreneurs Should Look for Meaning, Not Happiness." Originally published November 2015. Currently available online: https://www.inc.com/damon-brown/why-entrepreneurs-should-look-for-meaning-not-happiness.html

Brown, Damon. *Inc.*, "Best-Selling Author Adam Grant: The Most Highly Functional Companies Have These 3 Traits." Originally published February 2018. Currently available online: https://www.inc.com/damon-brown/according-to-adam-grant-one-word-highly-functional-workplaces-have-in-common-if-it-is-used-carefully.html

Brown, Damon. *The Ultimate Bite-Sized Entrepreneur Trilogy: 76 Ways to Boost Time, Productivity & Focus on Your Big Idea* (Bring Your Worth, 2017).

Jarvis, Chase. *Creative Calling: Establish a Daily Practice, Infuse Your World with Meaning, and Succeed in Work + Life* (Harper Business, 2019).

Hendricks, Gay. *The Big Leap: Conquer Your Hidden Fear and Take Life to the Next Level* (HarperOne, 2009).

Greene, Robert. *The 48 Laws of Power* (Penguin Books, 2000).

Brown, Damon. *Bring Your Worth: How to Level Up Your Creative Power, Value & Service to the World* (Bring Your Worth, 2017).

II. Uncover Power in Your Own Toolbox. Intro

Quora, "Do the roots of a tree go as deep as the tree is tall?" Originally published September 2019. Currently available online: https://www.quora.com/Do-the-roots-of-a-tree-go-as-deep-as-the-tree-is-tall

Godin, Seth. *The Practice: Shipping Creative Work* (Portfolio, 2020).

Recognize and Mine Your Biggest Established Strength

Merchant, Nilofer. *The Power of Onlyness: Make Your Wild Ideas Mighty Enough to Dent the World* (Viking, 2017).

Brown, Damon. *Build From Now: How to Know Your Power, See Your Abundance & Nourish the World* (Bring Your Worth, 2021).

Brown, Damon. #BringYourWorth show. "How to Fail Well (Brené Brown Quote)." Originally aired April 19, 2021. Available online: https://www.youtube.com/watch?v=LAl9Y30h--Q

Translate Past Power to Future Success

Merchant, Nilofer. *The Power of Onlyness: Make Your Wild Ideas Mighty Enough to Dent the World* (Viking, 2017).

Campbell, Joseph. *The Hero with a Thousand Faces* (The Collected Works of Joseph Campbell), 3rd ed. (New World Library, 2008)

Brown, Damon. *Build From Now: How to Know Your Power, See Your Abundance & Nourish the World* (Bring Your Worth, 2021).

Brown, Damon. *Bring Your Worth: How to Level Up Your Creative Power, Value & Service to the World* (Bring Your Worth, 2017).

Heath, Dan. *Upstream: The Quest to Solve Problems Before They Happen* (Avid Reader Press/Simon & Schuster, 2020).

Grant, Adam. *Give and Take: Why Helping Others Drives Our Success* (Orion, 2014).

Godin, Seth. *The Practice: Shipping Creative Work* (Portfolio, 2020).

Making Room for Your Wisdom

Godin, Seth. *The Practice: Shipping Creative Work* (Portfolio, 2020).

Newport, Cal. *A World Without Email: Reimaging Work in an Age of Communication Overload* (Portfolio, 2021).

Heath, Dan. *Upstream: The Quest to Solve Problems Before They Happen* (Avid Reader Press/Simon & Schuster, 2020).

Brown, Damon. *Bring Your Worth: How to Level Up Your Creative Power, Value & Service to the World* (Bring Your Worth, 2017).

Holiday, Ryan, and Stephen Hanselman. *The Daily Stoic: 366 Meditations on Wisdom, Perseverance, and the Art of Living* (Portfolio, 2016).

Brown, Damon. *Inc.*, "The Strongest Leaders Use This Simple, Powerful Phrase." Originally published May 2016. Currently available online: https://www.inc.com/damon-brown/the-strongest-leaders-use-this-simple-powerful-phrase-.html

Brown, Brené. *Rising Strong: How the Ability to Reset Transforms the Way We Live, Love, Parent, and Lead* (Random House, 2017).

III. Discover Economic Opportunities in the New World Order: Intro

Saporito, Bill. *Inc.*. "Steve Case Has Bet on Rust Belt Startups for Years. In the Pandemic, More VCs Have Joined Him" Originally published March 2021. Currently available online: https://www.inc.com/magazine/202104/bill-saporito/steve-case-rise-of-the-rest-midwest-cities-startup-hub-ecosystem.html

Assess the Business Landscape

Grant, Adam. *WorkLife with Adam Grant.* "How to Rethink a Bad Decision." Originally aired March 30, 2021. Transcript currently available online: https://www.ted.com/podcasts/worklife/how-to-rethink-a-bad-decision-transcript

Hurt, Jeanette. *Forbes*. "Texas Distillery Launches New Whiskey During Pandemic." Originally published June 30, 2020. Currently available online: https://www.forbes.com/sites/jeanettehurt/2020/06/30/texas-distillery-launches-new-whiskey-during-pandemic/?sh=75abb9a861b0

Parish, Shane. Instagram. Originally posted May 14, 2021. "A lot of errors happen when you try to speed up what's naturally going to happen. The lack of patience changes the outcome." Currently available online: https://www.instagram.com/p/CO3IwxrJ9ui/

Pivot Based on Worldly Circumstances

Hendricks, Gay. *The Big Leap: Conquer Your Hidden Fear and Take Life to the Next Level* (HarperOne, 2009).

Gilbert, Elizabeth. "Success, Failure, and the Drive to Keep Creating." (TED Talks. March 2014. Currently available online: https://www.ted.com/talks/elizabeth_gilbert_success_failure_and_the_drive_to_keep_creating/

Gritters, Jenni. Twitter. Posted June 25, 2021. https://twitter.com/jenni_gritters/status/1408535672139436032

Brown, Damon. *The Ultimate Bite-Sized Entrepreneur Trilogy: 76 Ways to Boost Time, Productivity & Focus on Your Big Idea* (Bring Your Worth, 2017).

B High Atl, "Wendy Day: 2pac, No Limit & Cash Money Deals, How to Make It in the Music Industry, Full Interview." Originally aired June 16, 2021. Currently available online: https://youtu.be/UKH-qTpJNNs

Strategize Your First Move and Ultimate Goals

Brown, Damon. *Inc.*, "Why Your Story Is the Secret to Your Success." Originally published August 2017. Currently available online: https://www.inc.com/damon-brown/why-your-story-is-the-secret-to-your-success.html

Covey, Stephen R. *7 Habits of Highly Effective People,* 30th Anniversary Ed.) (Simon & Schuster, 2020).

Blake, Jenny. *Pivot: The Only Move That Matters Is Your Next One* (Portfolio, 2017).

Brown, Damon. *Inc.*, "Best-Selling Author Adam Grant: The Most Highly Functional Companies Have These 3 Traits." Originally published February 2018. Currently available online: https://www.inc.com/damon-brown/according-to-adam-grant-one-word-highly-functional-workplaces-have-in-common-if-it-is-used-carefully.html

Kotter, John P. *Harvard Business Review,* "Leading Change: Why Transformation Efforts Fail." Originally published January 2007. Currently available online: https://hbr.org/2007/01/leading-change-why-transformation-efforts-fail

Aten, Jason. *Inc.*, "For Elon Musk, Everything Is a Side Project. Why That's Pure Emotional Intelligence." Originally published July 2021. Currently available online: https://www.inc.com/jason-aten/for-elon-musk-everything-is-a-side-project-why-thats-pure-emotional-intelligence.html

IV. Create Your Second Act: Intro

Adam Grant quote. Grant, Adam. LinkedIn. Originally published May 2021. Currently available online: https://www.linkedin.com/posts/adammgrant_if-youre-considering-a-career-change-but-activity-6803660302886989824-QeOx

Godin, Seth. *Akimbo* (podcast). Currently available online: http://www.akimbo.com

Brown, Damon. *Build From Now: How to Know Your Power, See Your Abundance & Nourish the World* (Bring Your Worth, 2021).

Brown, Damon. *Inc.*, "Why Your Day Job Is a Smart Investment." Originally published July 2019. Currently available online: https://www. inc.com/damon-brown/why-your-day-job-is-a-smart-investment.html

Brown, Damon, and Jeanette Hurt. *The Passive Writer: 5 Ways to Earn Money in Your Sleep* (Bring Your Worth, 2018).

Make Your Next Career Move

Brown, Damon. *Inc.*, "Best-Selling Author Adam Grant: The Most Highly Functional Companies Have These 3 Traits." Originally published February 2018. Currently available online: https://www.inc.com/ damon-brown/according-to-adam-grant-one-word-highly-functional-workplaces-have-in-common-if-it-is-used-carefully.html

Brown, Damon. *Inc.*, "The Ultimate Steve Jobs Quote for Taking Strong, Decisive Action." Originally published April 2016. Currently available online: https://www.inc.com/damon-brown/the-ultimate-steve-jobs-quote-for-taking-strong-decisive-action.html

Godin, Seth. *The Dip: A Little Book That Teaches You When to Quit (and When to Stick)* (Portfolio, 2007).

Brown, Damon. *The Ultimate Bite-Sized Entrepreneur Trilogy: 76 Ways to Boost Time, Productivity & Focus on Your Big Idea* (Bring Your Worth, 2017).

Brown, Damon. *Build From Now: How to Know Your Power, See Your Abundance & Nourish the World* (Bring Your Worth, 2021).

Sinek, Simon. *Start with Why: How Great Leaders Inspire Everyone to Take Action* (Portfolio, 2011).

Brown, Damon. *Inc.*, "How to Know It's Time to Leave Your Prominent Job." Originally published December 2019. Currently available online:

https://www.inc.com/damon-brown/how-to-know-its-time-to-leave-your-prominent-job.html

Brown, Damon. *The Forecast by Nutanix,* "The Power Couple Who Left Apple to Revolutionize IoT." Originally published September 2020. Currently available online: https://www.nutanix.com/theforecastbynutanix/profile/from-apple-to-new-iot-startup-humane

Brown, Damon. *Inc.,* "How Founders Create the Culture of the Companies They Build." Originally published March 2017. Currently available online: https://doi.org/10.1002/ltl.20292

Brown, Damon. *Inc.,* "How This Mother and Daughter Teamed Up to Become Social Entrepreneurs." Originally published December 2015. Currently available online: https://www.inc.com/damon-brown/why-mother-daughter-team-left-ogilvy-for-launch-humanitarian-app.html

Ries, Eric. *The Lean Startup: How Today's Entrepreneurs Use Continuous Innovation to Create Radically Successful Businesses* (Currency, 2011).

Greene, Robert. *The 48 Laws of Power* (Penguin Books, 2000).

Brown, Damon. *Inc.,* "How to Find the Most Passionate Employees." Originally published June 2017. Currently available online: https://www.inc.com/damon-brown/how-to-find-the-most-passionate-employees.html

Lean Into Steady Growth (Without Losing Your Shirt)

Brown, Damon. *Inc.,* "Why You Keep Falling into the Extreme Decision-Making Trap." Originally published August 2015. Currently available online: https://www.inc.com/damon-brown/why-you-keep-falling-into-the-extreme-decision-making-trap.html

Hendricks, Gay. *The Big Leap: Conquer Your Hidden Fear and Take Life to the Next Level* (HarperOne, 2009).

Brown, Damon. *Inc.*, "Why Even the Biggest Risk-Takers Need Some Stability." Originally published July 2015. Currently available online: https://www.inc.com/damon-brown/why-even-the-biggest-risk-takers-need-some-stability.html

Runcie, Dan. *Trapital,* "How Will and Jada Pinkett Smith Built a Content and Commerce Powerhouse." Originally published April 2021. Currently available online: https://trapital.co/2021/04/05/how-will-and-jada-pinkett-smith-built-a-content-and-commerce-powerhouse/

Collins, Jim. *Good to Great: Why Some Companies Make the Leap and Others Don't* (HarperBusiness, 2001).

Sims, Peter. *Little Bets: How Breakthrough Ideas Emerge from Small Discoveries* (Simon & Schuster, 2011).

Guillebeau, Chris. *Side Hustle: From Idea to Income in 27 Days* (Currency, 2017).

Vanderkam, Laura. *Juliet's School of Possibilities: A Little Story about the Power of Priorities* (Portfolio, 2019).

Brown, Damon. *Inc.*, "This Simple Time Formula Could Boost Your Business Growth." Originally published May 2019. Currently available online: https://www.inc.com/damon-brown/this-simple-time-formula-could-boost-your-business-growth.html

Brown, Damon. *The Ultimate Bite-Sized Entrepreneur Trilogy: 76 Ways to Boost Time, Productivity & Focus on Your Big Idea* (Bring Your Worth, 2017).

Brown, Damon. #BringYourWorth show. Available online: http://www.youtube.com/browndamon

Brown, Damon. #BringYourWorth boot camp. Available online: http://
paylancing.teachable.com

Measure Your Results and Adjust as Necessary
Skerrett, Patrick J. *Harvard Health Blog,* "Is Retirement Good
for Health or Bad for It?" Originally published December 2012.
Currently available online: https://www.health.harvard.edu/blog/
is-retirement-good-for-health-or-bad-for-it-201212105625

Brown, Damon. *Build From Now: How to Know Your Power, See Your
Abundance & Nourish the World* (Bring Your Worth, 2021).

Brown, Damon. *The Ultimate Bite-Sized Entrepreneur Trilogy: 76 Ways
to Boost Time, Productivity & Focus on Your Big Idea* (Bring Your Worth,
2017).

Brown, Damon. *Bring Your Worth: How to Level Up Your Creative Power,
Value & Service to the World* (Bring Your Worth, 2017).

Heath, Dan. *Upstream: The Quest to Solve Problems Before They Happen*
(Avid Reader Press/Simon & Schuster, 2020).

Goggins, David. Instagram, "There is not always a light at the end of the
tunnel . . ." Originally published July 11, 2021. Currently available online:
https://www.instagram.com/p/CRMykNFHQRp/

V. Build Alliances as You Create Your Best Business Brand: Intro
Rashad Bilal quote. Bilal, Rashad, Instagram. Originally published
May 2021. Currently available online: https://www.instagram.com/p/
CPTCXxIsUuI/

Brown, Damon. *Bring Your Worth: How to Level Up Your Creative Power,
Value & Service to the World* (Bring Your Worth, 2017).

Surbhi S. KeyDifferences.com, "Difference Between Transactional and Relationship Marketing." Originally published March 2020. Currently available online: https://keydifferences.com/difference-between-transactional-and-relationship-marketing.html

Blake, Jenny. *Pivot: The Only Move That Matters Is Your Next One* (Portfolio, 2017).

Brown, Damon. *Inc.*, "1 Reason You Should Network at Every Opportunity." Originally published March 2018. Currently available online: https://www.inc.com/damon-brown/the-real-reason-why-you-should-network.html

Brown, Damon. *Inc.*, "Why Most People Are Wealthy (And Don't Realize It)." Originally published February 2018. Currently available online: https://www.inc.com/damon-brown/why-waiting-on-money-is-blocking-your-true-success.html

Create Partnerships, Barterships, and Co-Signs

Clark, Dorie. *Harvard Business Review,* "Even Senior Executives Need a Side Hustle." Originally published November 2017. Currently available online: https://hbr.org/2017/11/even-senior-executives-need-a-side-hustle

Brown, Damon. *Inc.*, "1 Reason You Should Network at Every Opportunity." Originally published March 2018. Currently available online: https://www.inc.com/damon-brown/the-real-reason-why-you-should-network.html

Clark, Dorie. *Harvard Business Review,* "Start Networking with People Outside Your Industry." Originally published October 2016. Currently available online: https://hbr.org/2016/10/start-networking-with-people-outside-your-industry

Brown, Damon. *The Ultimate Bite-Sized Entrepreneur Trilogy: 76 Ways to Boost Time, Productivity & Focus on Your Big Idea* (Bring Your Worth, 2017).

Brown, Damon. *The Passive Writer: 5 Ways to Earn Money in Your Sleep* (Bring Your Worth, 2018).

Brown, Damon. *Inc.*, "The 3 Best Money Moves Bootstrappers Can Make for 2021." Originally published December 2020. Currently available online: https://www.inc.com/damon-brown/the-3-best-money-moves-bootstrappers-can-make-for-2021.html

Purple Fluorite. "#BringYourWorth featuring Damon Brown." Available online: https://purplefluorite.bandcamp.com

Violet Blue. *ZDNet,* "Silicon Valley's Race Problem." Originally published October 30, 2011. Currently available online: https://www.zdnet.com/article/silicon-valleys-race-problem/

Burkus, David. *Friend of a Friend . . . : Understanding the Hidden Networks That Can Transform Your Life and Your Career* (Houghton Mifflin Harcourt, 2018).

Greene, Robert. *The 48 Laws of Power* (Penguin Books, 2000).

Brown, Damon. *Inc.*, "Why Entrepreneurs Should Look for Meaning, Not Happiness." Originally published November 2015. Currently available online: https://www.inc.com/damon-brown/why-entrepreneurs-should-look-for-meaning-not-happiness.html

Brown, Damon. *Bring Your Worth: How to Level Up Your Creative Power, Value & Service to the World* (Bring Your Worth, 2017).

Consciously Cultivate Trusting Advocates to Bring into Your Game Plan

Brown, Damon. *Porn & Pong: How Grand Theft Auto, Tomb Raider and Other Sexy Games Changed Our Culture* (Feral House, 2008).

Brown, Damon. *Damon Brown's Simple Guide to the iPad* (Self-published, 2010).

Grant, Adam. *Give and Take: Why Helping Others Drives Our Success* (Orion, 2014).

Uzzi, Brian, and Shannon Dunlap. *Harvard Business Review,* "How to Build Your Network." Originally published December 2005. Currently available online: https://hbr.org/2005/12/how-to-build-your-network

Brown, Damon. Instagram, "You wouldn't have to 'move in silence' if you surrounded yourself with people that want to see you win." Originally published July 7, 2020. Currently available online: https://www.instagram.com/p/CCTYRkjpj-5/

Strategize with Others to Make the Biggest Impact

Sehgal, Kabir. *Harvard Business Review,* "Why You Should Have (at Least) Two Careers." Originally published April 25, 2017. Currently available online: https://hbr.org/2017/04/why-you-should-have-at-least-two-careers

Uzzi, Brian, and Shannon Dunlap. *Harvard Business Review,* "How to Build Your Network." Originally published December 2005. Currently available online: https://hbr.org/2005/12/how-to-build-your-network

Brown, Damon. *Bring Your Worth: How to Level Up Your Creative Power, Value & Service to the World* (Bring Your Worth, 2017).

Merchant, Nilofer. *The Power of Onlyness: Make Your Wild Ideas Mighty Enough to Dent the World* (Viking, 2017).

Brown, Damon. *Inc.*, "How to Make Your Ideas Successful. Hint: It's Not Grit." Originally published August 2017. Currently available online: https://www.inc.com/damon-brown/how-to-make-your-ideas-successful-hint-its-not-gri.html

Burkus, David. DavidBurkus.com, "How to Create Psychological Safety on Teams." Originally published March 2021. Currently available online: https://davidburkus.com/2021/03/how-to-create-psychological-safety-on-teams/

VI. Build Systems to Bulletproof Your Career: Intro

Nicholas, Chani. "Reading for Sagittarius Rising." Chani podcast. Originally aired July 5, 2021. Currently available online through the Chani app: http://www.chaninicolas.com

Sehgal, Kabir. *Harvard Business Review*, "Why You Should Have (at Least) Two Careers." Originally published April 25, 2017. Currently available online: https://hbr.org/2017/04/why-you-should-have-at-least-two-careers

Brown, Damon. *Inc.,* "Why You Should Have More Than One Career at the Same Time." Originally published February 28, 2018. Currently available online: https://www.inc.com/damon-brown/why-you-should-have-more-than-one-career-at-same-time.html

Godin, Seth. "Compared to What?" *Akimbo* podcast. Originally aired July 8, 2021. Currently available online: http://www.akimbo.com

Don't Work for Systems, But Have Systems Work for You

Heath, Dan. *Upstream: The Quest to Solve Problems Before They Happen* (Avid Reader Press/Simon & Schuster, 2020).

Lipman, Joanne. *Time,* "The Pandemic Revealed How Much We Hate Our Jobs. Now We Have a Chance to Reinvent Work." Originally published June 1, 2021. Currently available online: https://time.com/6051955/work-after-covid-19/

Brown, Damon. *Inc.,* "Why You Should Have More Than One Career at the Same Time." Originally published February 28, 2018. Currently available online: https://www.inc.com/damon-brown/why-you-should-have-more-than-one-career-at-same-time.html

Brown, Damon. *Bring Your Worth: How to Level Up Your Creative Power, Value & Service to the World* (Bring Your Worth, 2017).

Understanding Passive Income and Other Opportunities Available to All

Brown, Damon. *Inc.,* "Why You Should Have More Than One Career at the Same Time." Originally published February 28, 2018. Currently available online: https://www.inc.com/damon-brown/why-you-should-have-more-than-one-career-at-same-time.html

Brown, Damon, and Jeanette Hurt. *The Passive Writer: 5 Ways to Earn Money in Your Sleep* (Bring Your Worth, 2018).

Blake, Jenny. *Pivot: The Only Move That Matters Is Your Next One* (Portfolio, 2017).

Brown, Damon. *Inc.,* "How to Find Your Own Weakness and Overcome Your Blind Spot." Originally published September 6, 2019. Currently available online: https://www.inc.com/damon-brown/how-to-find-your-own-weakness-overcome-your-blind-spot.html

Jones, Debra. *NBC News,* "With No Tours or Live Shows, Musicians have Found Ways to Bridge the Gap Online." Originally published September 20, 2020. Currently available online: https://www.nbcnews.com/news/us-news/no-tours-or-live-shows-musicians-have-found-ways-bridge-n1240478

Building a Sustainable Approach to Your Career
Godin, Seth. *Akimbo* podcast, "The River of Time." Originally aired July 13, 2021. Currently available online: http://www.akimbo.com

Brown, Damon. *Inc.,* "This Is Simon Sinek's Guaranteed Secret to Success Most of Us Won't Do." Originally published July 2018. Currently available online: https://www.inc.com/damon-brown/this-is-simon-sineks-guaranteed-secret-to-success-most-of-us-wont-do.html

ACKNOWLEDGMENTS

Career Remix is my first collaboration with Sterling Publishing since launching my own independent imprint, *Bring Your Worth*. A decade after our hardcover hit, *Playboy's Greatest Covers*, it's good to see that we can still create magic together. Thanks to editors Wendy Williams and Kate Zimmermann for shepherding the project, and my longtime advocate Marilyn Allen for negotiating so everyone wins. Thank you to my *Bring Your Worth* imprint friends and colleagues, editor Jeanette Hurt, and cover designer Bec Loss, as well as to *Inc.* magazine's Laura Lorber and Mark Coatney, *Nutanix's The Forecast's* Ken Kaplan, and *Costco Connection's* Steve Fisher for supporting my serving non-traditional entrepreneurs.

Special thanks to Miles Davis's *Water Babies*, Bill Evans's *Undercurrent* and *On a Friday Evening (Live)*, Graham Nash's *Songs for Beginners*, David Axelrod's *Songs of Experience,* and Quincy Jones's *The Dude* for giving a wonderful soundtrack to my research.

All my love to Parul, Alec, Abhi, and Amar, Bernadette Johnson, Tony Howard, and David Brown, as well as to Raymond Johnson, Deirdra Bishop, and my SF CP crew, who have been along for this fantastic ride.

And this book is for my coaching clients, past and present, and those who have guided me. I hope *Career Remix* captures some of the gems you've passed on to me.

INDEX

ABOUT THE AUTHOR

Damon Brown helps side hustlers, solopreneurs, and other non-traditional creatives bloom. As a best-selling author, two-time startup founder, and four-time TED speaker, Damon co-founded the popular platonic connection app Cuddlr and led it to acquisition within a year, all while being the primary caregiver of his infant son. He now guides others through his one-on-one business coaching, *Inc.* magazine column, www.incdamonbrown.com, and *#BringYourWorth* show every Monday, Wednesday, and Friday, www.youtube.com/browndamon. Most recently, Damon was the first entrepreneur-in-residence at the Toledo Library.

His popular keynotes build a conversation around work–life balance, personal success, and supporting diverse talent. *Inc.*, Salesforce, and Google have hosted his in-person and off-site talks. You can watch his keynotes at www.damonbrown.net.

Career Remix is his twenty-sixth book.

His notable titles include *Build From Now: How to Know Your Power, See Your Abundance & Nourish the World* (Bring Your Worth Publishing, 2021), the best-selling *The Ultimate Bite-Sized Entrepreneur Trilogy* (Bring Your Worth Publishing, 2017), and the coffee-table book *Playboy's Greatest Covers* (Sterling Publishing, 2012).

You can catch Damon in *Playboy, Fast Company,* and *Costco Connection,* as well as at any locale that serves really spicy food. He lives in Las Vegas, Nevada, with his wife, two young sons, and countless bottles of hot sauce. Connect with him at www.JoinDamon.me or on Twitter/Instagram at @browndamon.